JACK STRAW

Stop whining and Start Writing

Copyright © 2025 by Jack Straw

All rights reserved. No part of this publication may be reproduced, stored or transmitted in any form or by any means, electronic, mechanical, photocopying, recording, scanning, or otherwise without written permission from the publisher. It is illegal to copy this book, post it to a website, or distribute it by any other means without permission.

First edition

This book was professionally typeset on Reedsy.
Find out more at reedsy.com

Contents

1. The Muse is a Liar, and So Are You — 1
2. "Your Life Is a Dumpster Fire of Stories" — 8
3. "The Write Stuff: Tools and Other Shit You Don't Need" — 18
4. "Procrastination: The Fine Art of Doing Nothing… — 29
5. "Writing While Old: The Pros and the Cons" — 40
6. "The Chapter Where You Start Panicking" — 52
7. "Self-Editing: Cutting the Crap You Fell in Love With" — 65
8. "Publish or Perish: The Harsh Reality" — 76
9. "Fame, Fortune, and the Absolute Lack Thereof" — 88
10. "The Epilogue You'll Skip Anyway" — 99

Introduction: "Who the Hell Do You Think You Are?"

So you woke up this morning, looked in the mirror, and said, "I'm gonna write a book." That's cute. You've only been alive for half a century—what's another couple of years wasted staring at a bank piece of paper, right? I mean, sure, you've got a few more years on the planet, but, hear that? The clock's ticking. I hate to tell you this, but you've got a shelf life. All of us do. It's there, you might not see it on your face in the mirror, check your side panels, it's in the fine print. So, if you're actually gonna do this, better get on with it. .

Let's be honest: for some people, writing a book sounds about as appealing as giving birth through a nasal passage. To them I say "take a break, Leave it to Beaver will be on shortly. But, here you are, reading this first chapter like you're about to embark on a literary pilgrimage, ready to produce *the Great American Novel*—except…. you're not. At least, probably not. Most of what you write will be subpar at best. But hey, you're just getting started and after all, at this point in your life, you've endured more cringe-worthy events than you can count. Another embarrassing moment or two won't kill you, hopefully.

Excuses Are Like Belly Buttons or other body parts we won't name here: Everyone's Got One

You're over 50, which means you've likely spent decades perfecting your favorite excuses:

- **"I don't have time."** You do. You're just not using it well. Come on, Andy Griffith is funny, but you've got Barney's lines memorized. Turn it off.
- **"I'm too old to start now."** This one's hilarious. You might be too old for some things, like lifting a car without a jack to change a tire, or lion taming or shit like that, but a pen just isn't that heavy and paper cuts are

pretty rare, so stop with the age thing.
- **"I'm not talented."** That's true of most people. Look at any media outlet. Some people are untalented almost to the point of being nauseating. Didn't stop them, did it?

Look, if you've survived this long, you already know life is basically a series of mildly tolerable events occasionally interrupted by frantic episodes of shit storms and hailstones. So adding "writing a book" to your to-do list really isn't that big of a leap. List it right between washing the car and trimming that toenail that keeps scratching your partner at night.

You've Got Baggage—Use It

You might be thinking, "I don't have any interesting stories." More bullshit. You've been on this planet for over ten lustrum (50 years). In that time, you've witnessed bizarre trends, questionable fashion choices (shoulder pads, purple hair?), and some truly terrible music (disco, disco, disco). You've met an endless stream of idiotic behaviour, attended countless weddings, funerals and sporting events. You've endured bosses who didn't know shit from shinola, relatives who tested your patience and borrowed your car, and a few late-night decisions that no one else in the whole world knows about….except for that one person.

Guess what? That's pure, unadulterated gold when it comes to writing. All those mistakes and mishaps are your twisted little stepping stones to storytelling glory. If you don't use them, you're wasting perfectly good comedic fodder.

Your Inner Critic: The Jerk in Your Head

By the time you hit 50, you probably have a permanent roommate in your mind—a smartass critic who says things like, "Who do you think you are, Stephen King?" or "This is garbage—nobody's gonna read this." Well, Stephen King didn't write *Carrie* by listening to some internal imp telling him it wasn't worth it. Well maybe he did, he kind of looks like an imp listener, but he wrote it anyway, and look what happened: a shower scene with pig's blood.

So yes, your internal critic will whisper sweet nothings about how awful you are. The trick is to shout back, "Shut the hell up! Don't make me come over there!" Because if you let that voice stop you, you'll never finish your book. Of course, I wouldn't shout this out loud if there are family members around. They might take your car keys away.

Why Writing This Book Is Your Destiny... Sort Of

You might not believe in destiny, but you probably believe in regret. Regret can be a tough deal. And here's the thing: not writing the book you've been yammering about for years will add one more regret to your growing list. You don't have time for that. At your age, you've got fewer excuses and even less patience for B.S. So you might as well funnel all that frustration and wisdom (or whatever) into something tangible.

Think of this as giving your future self a reason to say, "At least I tried." Because let's face it, most people don't even earn the right to say that.

1

The Muse is a Liar, and So Are You

Look, let's get something out in the open right from the start: This so-called "muse" everyone keeps blabbering about? You know, the sudden and dramatic inspiration? It doesn't exist. Not really. She's not some tiny winged topless fairy floating around, waiting to bless you with creative brilliance the moment you light a scented candle and put on your new writing specs. That's all horse crap. The muse is nothing more than a convenient lie we tell ourselves when we're feeling too damn lazy, or we're just too full of excuses to actually start writing. "Oh, I'm waiting for inspiration or I'm waiting for the right mood," you say, perched atop your plush desk chair, sipping the suds off a cold beer and checking out crucially important Facebook posts from Gloria the gossip queen on your phone. Waiting for inspiration? Yeah, sure you are. And I'm waiting for my neighbor's lizard Jerome to deliver a pizza. Both scenarios have about the same probability of coming true.

But here's the real kicker: We *want* to believe in the muse. It's such a comforting idea, isn't it? The thought that there's some unseen creative force just itching to sprinkle a little magic dust on our keyboard or notepad, allowing words to flow effortlessly from our brain. If that were true, writing a book would be as simple as waiting for the creative stork to drop off a fully formed manuscript on your doorstep. Reality is much different. The stork's dead, the muse is a phony, and all you've got is your brain, your fingers, and your willingness to say, "Screw it, I'm writing anyway."

Now, don't get me wrong: Inspiration can strike. Sometimes you might wake up from a bizarre dream involving your cousin Earl riding a three-legged unicorn naked down Wall Street, and suddenly you've got the kernel of an idea for the next big thriller. Or maybe you'll be vacuuming your living room, or prying what you hope is just a Milk Dud out of your grandson's hair, and *bam*—a line of dialogue pops into your head that's too good to ignore. Those moments are awesome. They feel like gifts from above. But waiting around for them is like waiting for Ronnie Howard to show up offering you a starring role in his next movie. Besides, that picture of Earl in all his stretch marked glory could be hard to escape.

Let's face it: if you're over 50, you've had untold years of practice lying to yourself about a whole range of things—your diet, your exercise routine, how well you sing Bohemian Rhapsody—so why should writing be any different? We spin these little yarns in our heads about how one day, the universe will just align and everything will fall into place. The kids will be quiet, the spouse will be occupied, the dog will walk itself, and the words will flow like beer at a senior keg. Except that's not how it ever works. If you've learned anything in your time on this planet, it's that the universe is too damn busy with asteroids and black holes to give a shit about you.

The truth is, writing is a discipline. Kind of like working out, except without the sweat, usually. It's not a mystical experience and it's not some 1960's flashback from some ill advised acid trip. Besides, unless you're a lot older than 50 that wouldn't happen. If you are old enough, more power to you. It's also not some cosmic event that requires astrological charts and favorable lunar phases. It's sitting your butt in a chair—even when you don't feel like it—and plunking out words one at a time. Sometimes they'll be good words. Sometimes they'll be garbage. But if you don't write the garbage, you'll never sift your way to the gold. It's like panning for gold in a river full of mud. You're going to get dirty, and you're going to find a whole lot of rocks that aren't worth squat. But every once in a while, you'll spot that little glimmer, and that's when it starts to come together.

Of course, it's so much easier to say, "I don't feel inspired right now." That's basically code for "I'd rather take a nap." We all get it. Modern life offers countless ways to avoid doing anything productive: streaming services with endless shows, social media platforms that feed us dopamine hits every time we see a cat video, and let's not forget the ever valuable TV shopping networks. You can spend hours hunting for the perfect pair of socks, then wonder where your entire afternoon went. Meanwhile, your supposed "muse" is quietly sitting in the corner, laughing at your gullibility.

You see, the muse is not only a liar, but a tempting little scapegoat. We love to blame her for our own shortcomings. Didn't write anything today? "Oh, I just wasn't inspired." Couldn't finish that chapter? "I guess the muse took a day off." Word of advice: stop delegating your creativity to a mythical figure. If you didn't write, it's because you didn't *choose* to write. It had nothing to do with the alignment of the stars or the performance of your morning yoga routine. You either sat down and wrote, or you didn't. End of story.

Now, let's talk about the second part of this delightful chapter title: *And So Are You*. Because if the muse is a liar, guess what? So are you. We all are, to some degree. We lie to ourselves about why we haven't finished that short story, or that novel, or why we haven't fixed that damn garbage disposal that hasn't worked since you dropped the shot glass into it three birthday parties ago. We claim we're too busy, too old, too tired, or too unworthy. Bury that stuff in that box in the corner where your cat relieves herself. If you really, truly want to do something, you'll find the time. You made time to argue with your dumbass brother-in-law about how Michael is better than LeBron, didn't you? Or how about the day you laid on the couch and consumed a whole bag of barbecue chips and chocolate milk? You found time for that.

But writing? Oh no, that's too hard. Too demanding. Too much effort without guarantees. Yes, writing requires confrontation with your own mind. You can't just coast through it. You have to face your flaws, your insecurities, and your dumb-ass ideas head-on. And that's scary. It's much simpler to wait for just the right mood to come along. That way, if nothing gets written, you can blame the mood for not showing up, instead of admitting that *you* were the one who failed to put in the effort. I'm talking to you. Yeah, you there on the couch.

Here's a little secret: once you stop waiting, you might find that something like genuine inspiration can show up more often. Not because the inspiration finally decided you were worthy, but because you're training your brain to be on the lookout. When you make writing a consistent practice—whether it's an hour each morning, thirty minutes during your lunch break, or late at night after the family's gone to bed—you prime your mind to generate ideas. In other words, you're telling your subconscious, "Alright, we're serious about this shit. It's time to get to work." And guess what? Your subconscious usually listens if you keep at it.

But if you only try to write when you "feel like it," you'll end up writing as often as a politician tells the truth—which throughout history has only happened once, but no one remembers when it was. Sure, there might be moments of spontaneous brilliance that show up once in a blue moon, but that won't get a book finished. It won't even get a short story finished. You need consistency. You need to push through on the days you'd rather do anything else. You need to treat writing like a job. And if you're over 50, you've probably had a job or two in your life. You know that if you showed up only when you felt like it, you'd have been fired in a heartbeat. Maybe not these days, but there was a time that was true.

Now, maybe you're still not convinced. You're thinking, "But I'm special. I *need* my inspiration. Without it, I'm just forcing it." Don't be so damn needy. This isn't a time for hugs and hair strokes. Writing doesn't care about your comfort level. And forcing it? Of course you have to force it sometimes. That's the nature of creating something out of nothing. If it were easy, your entire family and a couple of retired former coworkers would be dressed like Hemingway, half drunk on an island somewhere, living on royalties and signing autographs for tourists.

Besides, forcing it isn't necessarily a bad thing. Think of it this way: remember the first time you tried to do something challenging—like ride a bike or yodel or try to smooch with that cute classmate at the homecoming dance? It didn't come naturally, did it? You probably skinned your knees, damaged your nasal passages and got turned down cold. But you kept at it. You forced it until it started feeling natural. Except the yodelling, of course. Writing works the same way. You wrestle with the blank page, you yell at your laptop, you produce awful sentences you're embarrassed to read. Then, suddenly, you get a paragraph that's actually pretty good. And another. And before you know it, you're on a roll. After all, didn't that cute classmate end up marrying you? No? Oh well.....

Still not sure? Here's a reality check: if you keep lying to yourself, you'll never write anything. You'll remain one of those people who walk around proudly announcing, "I have this great idea for a book," but never produce a single chapter. Folks hear that and nod politely, but internally they're rolling their eyes, because guess what? Everyone's got an idea for a book. Ideas are cheap, in fact in most places they're free. Execution is the real currency.

Let's not forget another sneaky little lie we tell ourselves: "I'm too old to start now." Give me a break. You're not too old to start anything except maybe trying out for the Olympic gymnastics team. But writing? Age could actually be your biggest asset. You've lived. You've seen things. You've got stories to tell—ridiculous family reunions, workplace disasters, personal triumphs, heartaches, and a thousand random occurrences that can spark interesting, relatable writing. So, if you're gonna lie to yourself, at least pick a lie that doesn't sabotage your creativity. But, if you ever decide to try that Olympic thing, do two things: video the session and send it to me. I have to see that.

Think about this, do you want to end up on your deathbed thinking, "I should've written that book, but I never took the time." That's pathetic. It's like saying you should've gone outside more, but the sun never personally invited you. Stop waiting for invitations and start sending them out yourself. Your writing desk is the party. The muse is free to drop by if it wants, but the festivities go on with or without it.

So, yes, the muse is a liar—a figment of your imagination conjured up to shift responsibility away from you. And you're a liar, too, every time you claim you can't write because you're not feeling that mystical "creative spark." Deep down, you know it's just fear talking. Fear that your work won't be good enough, or that you'll run out of steam, or that nobody will read it. But here's the thing: those fears are normal. Every writer deals with them. The difference is, successful writers write anyway. They live and thrive in the outhouse of doubt. They push through the shitstorm of insecurity. They show up, day after day, even when the muse is AWOL, and they hammer out the words.

And that's what you've got to do. Stop lying to yourself about needing perfect conditions, an ideal mental state, or cosmic alignment. The best time to write is now, when you're reading this sentence and thinking, "Hey, maybe I should dig through the couch cushions and find a pen." Because guess what? You're not getting any younger, and the world certainly isn't getting any saner. If you've got something to say, spit it out already. Write it down, let it be messy, let it be flawed, let it be downright awful at first. You can always fix it later. But you can't fix a blank page.

Now, you might be wondering if this entire chapter is just one long guilt trip designed to make you feel bad about not writing. Bingo. That's exactly what it is. And you *should* feel a little guilty if you've spent the last fifty years or more talking about writing but never actually doing it. Guilt can be a great motivator—just ask anyone who's tried to diet during the holidays. The key is to channel that guilt into action. Turn it into a reason to put words on the page, to rewrite them when they suck, and to keep going until you've got something you're proud of—or at least something that doesn't make you want to put on a disguise, change your name and move to a small town in Arkansas.

Now, you should have no doubt. So, the next time you feel the urge to say, "I'm waiting for inspiration," do yourself a favor: call it what it is. You're stalling. You're hesitating. You're letting fear dictate your actions. Instead, sit down, open that blank page, and start writing. It doesn't matter if you write your to-do list, a rant about your neighbor's barking dog, or the opening line of the next Great American Novel. Just write something. Anything. Because, once you're in motion, you're far more likely to stay in motion. Here's an idea. When was the last time you wrote a letter? To anyone? That's a form of writing and good practice. Maybe write a letter to someone to inform them that they are the first person you are officially notifying that you are going to write a book. Pick someone who would be supportive or at least a big pain in the ass if you falter at your task, either will work.

And that, my friend, is how you conquer the lying muse and the liar within yourself. You pick up the pen (or tap the keyboard), and you write. You keep writing until the muse has no choice but to follow your lead—if it ever shows up at all. And if it doesn't? Who cares? Because you're the one creating the words, not her. You're the one with decades of living under your belt, with stories waiting to be told. You're the one in control, and ultimately, you're the one who'll get credit for every sentence that makes it to the page.

So, stop with the excuses, stop waiting, and start writing. The muse can stay locked in the closet for all we care. This is your book, your story, your words. Enter the messy world of multiple typos and crappy penmanship. That's where the real magic lies—not in some mythological muse, but in your willingness to show up and do the work. Because at the end of the day, that's the only thing that separates a writer from a wannabe.

Welcome to the life of creating. It's not pretty, it's not neat, but it's absolutely worth it. Now get your ass to work.

2

"Your Life Is a Dumpster Fire of Stories"

Let's get one thing straight: Your life is not a neat, polished fable bursting with moral lessons and heartwarming endings. On the other hand, if it is you might as well find something else to do because no one's gonna give a shit about that story. Your life is a dumpster fire, at least part of it is—and that's fantastic news for your book. "But wait," you might say, "my life isn't *that* bad." Ah, denial—truly the greatest of human coping mechanisms. I'm not saying you're on the verge of living under a freeway underpass (although if you are, that's a hell of a story). I'm just pointing out that if you're over 50, you've got multiple years worth of chaotic episodes to draw upon. That's a mountain of comedic, dramatic, and downright bizarre content, all begging to be turned into something worth reading.

If you think your life's a pristine fairytale, you're either lying to yourself or you're unbelievably boring. Nobody's life is that perfect, and if it were, it wouldn't make for interesting reading anyway. People love dumpster fires. They slow down to watch car wrecks, they binge-watch reality shows featuring grown adults flipping tables, and they revel in the melodrama of social media blowouts. As a writer, you've got to tap into that universal fascination with disaster. Because guess what? You've personally survived countless minor (and maybe major) catastrophes. And each one is a story waiting to happen.

1. Identifying Your Dumpster Fires

You know how actual dumpster fires start, right? Usually from someone tossing a smoldering cigarette or lighting junk on fire for kicks. Life's not so different. Something small—like a missed payment, a forgotten appointment, or a miscommunication—can spiral out of control and *poof*, you find yourself knee-deep in a conflagration of your own making. But hey, you lived to tell the tale. That's the key phrase: *tell the tale.*

Maybe it was that disastrous first marriage that ended in a flurry of resentment and expensive lawyers and custody battles over Cletus, the thousand five thousand dollar Shih Tzu . Or the time you almost lost your job when you overindulged in the ale at the office Christmas party and told your boss his wife might not be so bitchy if she lost a few of the pounds she seemed to keep finding. Or how about the time you decided to set your son down and tell him about the birds and the bees and he told you about condoms and orgasms. All these fiascos, big and small, can be molded into mesmerizing stories—if you're willing to be honest about them. The gold is often buried in the stuff we'd rather forget, but that's precisely the territory you need to mine.

The trick is to reframe these personal train wrecks. Instead of labeling them as "the worst day of my life," think of them as "the day my life gave me top shelf writing material." Because let's face it, nobody wants to read about the day everything went smoothly. That's a Hallmark card, not a story.

2. Embrace the Cringe

Sometimes writing is all about pointing out how absurd our lives really are. The mismatch between how we like to present ourselves—polished, put-together, *normal*—and how we actually live—confused, messy, riddled with missteps—is a comedic goldmine. You've done embarrassing things. Admit it. Perhaps you showed up at a fancy event with toilet paper stuck to your shoe. Maybe you called your new significant other by your ex's name (always a fun time). Or you once gave a presentation at work with your fly undone. Each humiliating moment is a potential comedic anecdote.

Here's the secret: people *love* multicolored messes of the highest order. They love reading about awkward, embarrassing failures because it reminds them they're not alone in their own humiliations. Sharing these stories bonds you with your readers. You're saying, "Look, I'm human, I mess up, and it's ridiculous—laugh with me." That's exactly the kind of authenticity that keeps readers turning pages. They want to see how you coped, how you survived the mortification, and what you learned—which was probably very little, but no matter, it's worth reading.

When you write, don't skip over and do not sanitize the mess. Lean into it. Describe every excruciating detail: the sweat pooling on your forehead, the stammering, the wide-eyed horror as you realized you just texted the wrong person. The more vividly you paint the scene, the more memorable it becomes. And guess what? The more memorable it is, the more likely your readers will share it with friends, turning your little dumpster fire into a viral inferno of laugh-inducing delight.

3. Mining Relationships for Chaos

Nothing provides endless narrative fuel quite like other people. Spouses, ex-spouses, children, parents, siblings, best friends, frenemies—each one of them is a walking, talking subplot. If you're over 50, you've likely accumulated a variety of relationships that have run the gamut from blissful to toxic. Maybe you've got a brother who still owes you money from 1987, or a cousin who shows up unannounced every Thanksgiving and criticizes your gravy. All that drama is story gold.

The challenge, of course, is how to write about these folks without starting a family feud. My advice? Don't worry about it too much—yet. Get the stories down first. You can always soften the edges or change names later. Because if you censor yourself from the get-go, you're essentially strangling your creativity with one hand and covering its mouth with the other. Write first, worry about consequences second. After all, these people gave you these stories by existing in your life. The least they can do is let you profit—artistically, if not financially—from their antics. Maybe your brother will be shamed into paying you back and your cousin will learn to not be such an asshole. Or maybe he'll be worse. That's life and that's writing.

Remember that the best relationship stories often revolve around conflict.

Nobody wants to hear about the time you and your spouse watched Netflix in peace, holding hands and gently chuckling at a sitcom. Snore. They want to hear about the time you and your spouse got carried away during an adult movie viewing and started rolling around on the carpet only to have your daughter's new St. Bernard puppy, believing an attack is in progress, dash in to rescue your partner by nipping at you in some areas that shouldn't be dog nipped, causing a trip to the emergency room where doctors laughed and nurses giggled between antiseptic, stitches and gauze applications. That's human drama—painful in the moment, hilarious in hindsight.

4. Harnessing the Power of Regret

By the time you reach 50, you've racked up enough regrets to fill a U-Haul truck or at least a large set of carry-on luggage. We're talking about those life decisions that make you cringe so hard your back spasms. "Why did I stay at that job for so long?" "Why did I trust that shady investment tip from my neighbor?" "Why the hell did I ever think playing strip Yahtzee with the plumber was a good idea?" Guess what: each regret is a prime candidate for a story.

Regrets often come with a certain gravitational pull. They nag at you, bouncing around in your skull like a pinball. Write about them. Explore the what ifs, the whys, and the hows. Be brutally honest. Did you cling to a relationship out of fear of being alone? Did you choose a career path because you wanted to impress someone? Did you miss out on an opportunity because you were too anxious to take a risk? Lay it all out. People relate to regrets because they have their own. And seeing someone else's regrets—especially presented with wit and brutal honesty—can be oddly comforting.

Plus, regrets often include a built-in arc: you did something, it went sideways, and now you're looking back with a newfound perspective. That's story structure 101: a beginning, middle, and end. The more cringe-worthy and emotional, the better. Don't hold back. Let it rip.

5. The Comedy in Catastrophe

A dumpster fire can be tragic, but it can also be really, really funny. A writer I know famously talked about how people find humor in tragedy—so long as it's happening to someone else. But even your own tragedies can become comedic fodder once you're safely removed from them by time. The heartbreak that gutted you at 27 might be downright hilarious when you're 57 and happily remarried. The job layoff that once felt like the end of the world might now seem like a comedic sideshow in the grand scheme of your life.

What's vital is your willingness to laugh at your own pain. Laughing at your misfortunes doesn't diminish them; it transforms them into something bigger than just misery. Laughter reclaims power over the memory. Instead of letting it haunt you, you're using it. It's like watching a show in your brain and saying, "Shit, I thought that was gonna screw me for life, but I can turn this into some seriously funny stuff." All you do is take what's painful, find the absurdity, and fling it back at the universe.

This approach doesn't mean you have to joke about everything. Some dumpster fires are too raw or too sensitive to spin into humor right away. But if you've had enough time to process something and find a comedic angle, go for it. Or, maybe, relate it in a serious way. Just don't be whiny, needy or self-sympathetic. Readers appreciate a narrator who can be both candid and lighthearted about life's messes. Don't cry in your oatmeal. It's a balancing act, sure, but when done right, it's magic.

6. Don't Sanitize Your Dumpster

Let's face it: some parts of your life are messy. You've probably been through a divorce or two, maybe had a bankruptcy scare, or maybe loaned a woman from South Carolina named Sheila you met on a dating site $500, only to find out it was actually a dude named Abimbola from Nigeria (and no, ol' Abimbola ain't paying you back). These experiences might still stir up shame or embarrassment. And yet, those are exactly the raw, messy bits that make for gripping reading.

In writing, authenticity is king. If you try to gloss over the gritty parts or sugarcoat them, readers will smell the deception a mile away. People can tell when you're tiptoeing around an uncomfortable truth. They want you to wade right into the middle of that dumpster fire, take a big whiff of the smoke, and describe how it makes your eyes water. Only then do they believe you. Only then do they trust you as a storyteller.

This doesn't mean you need to reveal your entire medical history or the intimate details of your darkest traumas. Boundaries still matter. But if a story has real potential—if it's genuinely part of who you are, and it shaped you—don't be afraid to go there. The risk often pays off in a powerful, memorable narrative.

7. Turning Victories into Stories, Too

You might think the only material worth writing about is your string of failures, but that's not entirely true. Yes, failures and flops are comedic catnip, but your victories can be just as intriguing—especially if they came at the tail end of a near disaster. Maybe you fought tooth and nail for a promotion you never thought you'd get. Maybe you finally confronted that toxic family member after years of tension. Or you learned to pilot a plane at 55, proving that yes, you can still do new things without spontaneously combusting.

The key to making triumphs engaging is to acknowledge the stumbles that preceded them. Nobody wants to read a brag-fest about how everything came easy. Show the process, the mess, and the frustration. Show how you almost gave up, how you questioned your sanity, and then, at the eleventh hour, pulled off a win that shocked even you. That's compelling. That's real. And that's exactly what your readers need to hear, because they're probably in the middle of their own dumpster fires, desperately hoping for a spark of hope that maybe, just maybe, they can come out on top too.

8. Channeling Your Inner Curmudgeon

If you're over 50, you've earned the right to be a bit of a curmudgeon now and then. Some writers are masters of curmudgeonly humor—spotlighting the inane stupidity of everyday life with brutal honesty. If you look around, you'll see plenty of material: the bizarre behaviors of your neighbors, the endless bureaucratic red tape that reduces any sane person to a seething mass of fury, the technological frustrations that come with each new remote control with too damn many buttons and functions.

Let that curmudgeonly perspective shine through in your writing. Rant about the things that drive you nuts. Complain, moan, exasperate—so long as you do it with wit and style, people will love it. There's a catharsis in seeing your frustrations mirrored on the page, especially when it's done with comedic flair. Just be sure to aim your ire in multiple directions—if you only harp on one topic, it can get stale. Spread that venom around. Humanity has given you an endless smorgasbord of stupidity to critique.

9. The Stories You Haven't Told Anyone

We all have secrets. By 50, you might be sitting on a treasure trove of them—stories you've never shared because you were worried about judgment, or you didn't think they mattered. But those secrets can be some of the most potent writing material out there. They're vulnerable, raw, and real. If you've spent half a century hiding them, think about what it would mean to finally let them out into the open—on your own terms, in your own words.

Some secrets are silly—like that time you accidentally shoplifted a candy bar and were too mortified to go back and pay for it. Others might be bigger—like a past relationship nobody in your current circle knows about, or a dream you abandoned because you were told it was impossible. Writing about these undisclosed parts of your life can be terrifying. But terror often precedes profound creative breakthroughs. Don't hold back; address the unspeakable topics nobody else wants to touch. Scary, huh? You don't have to go full throttle if it doesn't feel right but consider sipping from the bottle that holds the secret whiskey. Sometimes, the stories you're most afraid to tell are the ones people need to hear the most.

10. Making Sense of the Garbage Pile

Now, you might be thinking, "Great, I've got a ton of crazy ass stories. But how the hell do I shape them into a cohesive book?" That's where storytelling craft comes in. It's not enough to just vomit all your embarrassing anecdotes onto the page in a random sequence. You need to find threads, patterns, and themes. Ask yourself: Is there an overarching message or lesson tying these stories together? Maybe it's about resilience, or learning to laugh at yourself, or discovering that it's never too late to start over.

If you step back and look at your life from a bird's-eye view, you'll start seeing arcs. For instance, your repeated failures at relationships might be connected to a fear of vulnerability that started in childhood. (Is that some deep shit or what?) Or your catastrophes with money might stem from a single misguided belief that you never questioned until you were 48. Find those arcs and shape your stories around them. A dumpster fire still needs structure to keep readers engaged.

Remember, too, that you can weave humor throughout even the darkest tales. Comedy doesn't cancel out seriousness; it enhances it. It's that little spark in the darkness that makes readers keep flipping pages. Tackle heavy subjects—politics, religion, social issues—but do it by shining a light on the absurdity of it all. Apply the same principle to your own tales: highlight the ridiculous aspects of your biggest failures, call out the nonsensical rules you broke (or followed), and show how you eventually found your way out (or didn't).

11. Owning the Dumpster Fire

Ultimately, this chapter is about embracing the full scope of your life's chaos. Don't apologize for it. Don't downplay it. Own it. Write from a place of unabashed honesty. Because here's the kicker: You're not alone. Everyone's life has some crazy unexplainable and bizarre elements—most folks are just too chicken to admit it. By putting it all on the page, you're doing something both brave and oddly generous. You're giving readers permission to acknowledge their own fantastic fumbles without shame.

When you own your bonfire of lunacy, you transform it into a beacon for others wandering around with their own smoldering piles of regret, embarrassment, and missed opportunities. "Hey, look," you say. "I've been burned by my own stupidity and somehow survived. A little scarred but almost as pretty as I was in the beginning." That's powerful. That's compelling. And that's exactly what can make your writing resonate with people.

At the end of the day, you're turning life's messes into stories that matter. And whether you realize it or not, that's a gift. It's a gift to yourself—because writing this stuff down helps you process it, find humor in it, and potentially move on. And it's a gift to anyone who reads it, because they get to see themselves reflected in your dumpster fires, laugh at the absurdity, and perhaps feel a little less alone.

12. Let the Fire Burn

So, yes, your life is a dumpster fire. Congratulations. Instead of spending time trying to douse the flames, keep fanning them—on the page, anyway. Stoke the embers of your embarrassing moments, your regrets, your weird family dynamics, and your questionable life choices. Let it all ignite into a blaze of authenticity and wit. Because that's where the best writing comes from: the raw, unfiltered truth of our own chaotic existence.

Don't be afraid to poke around in the ashes, sifting through the charred remains of that old job, that relationship that imploded, or that humiliating fiasco you swore you'd never mention again. In those embers lie the stories that no one else can tell but you. And if you do it right—bring the candor and humor to the table—you might just craft something that makes readers laugh, cringe, and reflect all at once.

The world doesn't need another sanitized, feel-good yarn about how everything always works out. The world needs more stories that say, "Yeah, things got really bad, but I'm still here—and guess what, it's kind of hilarious in hindsight." If you can deliver that, you'll have readers nodding, smirking, and maybe even tearfully connecting with your experiences.

So go on. Torch that trash. Dance around the flames. Write your unvarnished truth. Because in this chapter—and throughout the rest of this book—the dumpster fire of your life is the main event. And let me tell you, there's nothing more entertaining than watching something burn when you know it's eventually going to give way to something better, or at least something you can laugh about. That's the real magic of writing about your old mistakes and blunders: turning pain into punchlines, regrets into revelations, and utter chaos into a compelling read.

In Closing

If Chapter One taught you that the muse is a liar (and so are you), Chapter Two is here to remind you that even if you *were* telling the truth, it'd still involve a hell of a lot of disarray and stupidity. So, why not grab it by the asscheeks and hang on? Accept that your life is a glorious, boiling volcano filled with the lava of cringe, conflict, and catastrophes—and be grateful. Because each flaming fragment is another sentence, paragraph or chapter in the story of....whatever the hell your story is called.

And you've got 50+ years of these little building blocks, don't you? Stop pretending everything's well-oiled and in perfect running order. No one believes that. Do you believe that? No? Good, at least we agree. So, grab the imaginary bucket and start sifting through the trash, gathering the best scraps, and piecing them together into something that just might set your readers' minds ablaze. That's the real secret to writing after 50: you've simply got more—and more varied—garbage to work with. See? Your life is garbage. Don't take it personal for god's sake. Use it. Because once you do, you'll realize that the real fuel for your writing isn't some mystical muse: it's your own messy, absurd, occasionally devastating life. And, paradoxically, that's where the true beauty lies—in transforming the detritus of everyday existence into stories that illuminate, entertain, and maybe even heal.

Bottom line? If you're looking for a neat and tidy roadmap to writing your first book, you're not going to find it here. What you'll find instead is a big sign that says: **"Your Life Is a Dumpster Fire—Now Go Make a Bonfire Out of It."** And that's exactly what you should do. Because fires are endlessly fascinating, especially when you're the one holding the match.

So, here's to the chaos that got you this far—and the stories it's about to unleash. Keep your eyes open, your pen handy, and let the sparks fly. Because in this world of never-ending nonsense, turning your personal chaos into compelling prose is just about the sanest move you can make. And who knows? Maybe once the smoke clears, you'll find something resembling meaning in the ashes. Or at least a good punchline. Either way, keep writing—you've got an inferno of stories to share.

3

"The Write Stuff: Tools and Other Shit You Don't Need"

Let's talk about gadgets, gizmos, and the modern-day obsession with *stuff*. In the old days, writers used quills, parchment, and possibly a swig of whiskey, and it was cheap whiskey at that. Now, you've got a thousand apps for "mind-mapping your creative process," software that checks your grammar, and fancy notebooks that promise to unlock your inner genius if you just spend the cash. You've even got "smart pens" that record your every scribble, because lord forbid you let a single half-baked idea slip away. All this noise, all this marketing, all these well-intentioned "productivity hacks," and do you know what they mostly do? They give you one more excuse not to write while you spend money on crap that justifies your stalling. "I can't start my book until I buy that special $300 writing app!" Right. And I can't let my bowels do their job until I get that new silky smooth 4 ply and someone to hold my hand. Okay, maybe not a great comparison, but you get the point.

I'll try to be fair: Humans love *stuff*. We collect it, display it, brag about it, and often let it define us. "I'm a deep creative kind of writer," you might say, as though that alone elevates your scribbles to Pulitzer material. Or "I can only write if the software is distraction-free, with a black background and green text, to simulate an old-school CRT." You see that? Just thinking about these so-called *requirements* is enough to push your writing session back another few days, maybe weeks, hell, maybe forever if you keep browsing for more. Eventually, you'll look around at your mountain of gear and realize you still haven't written one lousy chapter. That's why this book is all about unmasking nonsense, and Chapter Three sets its sights on the biggest con job in writing: the myth that you need more *stuff* to create.

1. The Mirage of the Perfect Writing Environment

Close your eyes for a second—after you're done reading this sentence. Picture your dream writing space. Go on, do it. Maybe you're envisioning a clean, minimalist desk overlooking a serene lake. A perfect cappuccino sits to your right, its latte art intact, never cooling. Birds chirp in the distance, providing a gentle soundtrack to your day. In this fantasy, the words just pour out of you, effortlessly, like some mystical fountain of literary genius. Everything is wonderful, *and you've* lost ten pounds overnight.

Now, snap back to reality. You're sitting at the kitchen table piled high with junk mail, last night's dishes, while you drink from a coffee cup you haven't washed since Noah launched his ark while you stare out the window at a passerby whose dog is defecating in your front yard with no sign that the handler is going to remove the evidence. Or maybe you have an actual office. You know the kind that you share with a spouse who loves to blare KC and the Sunshine Band hits (and yes they did have hits, don't blame me) until your creative side is turning to a mist and floating down the hall. Look, if you're waiting for perfection in your environment, you're going to be waiting a long time. Perfect conditions are a mirage, a convenient little daydream that you'll use to justify not writing.

Sure, there are small things you can do to make your space more tolerable—tidy up a bit, wear noise-cancelling headphones, and maybe close the curtains before the next dog walks by. But if your main excuse is "I just don't have the right writing environment," you're doing more daydreaming than writing. My Uncle L.Roy Crow would say, "Don't be an ass." Of course Uncle L.Roy said "Don't be an ass" in response to most comments, but in this case it means all you need is a place where you can sit, open a document, and type words without suddenly getting the urge to start disco spinning to "I'm Your Boogie

Man". Anything else is optional.

2. The Software Circus: Apps, Apps, and More Apps

Let's tackle the digital realm, because a freaking circus out there. You've got writing apps that promise to solve your writer's block, grammar apps that beep at you every time you split an infinitive, and plotting tools with more color-coded features than a NASA control panel. Don't get me wrong—some software can be genuinely helpful. But too many people turn the hunt for the *perfect* app into a procrastination marathon.

They install one program, tinker with it, and decide it's not quite right because the text doesn't display in Comic Sans (hey, some folks get into shit like that). Then they move on to the next piece of software, convinced that this time, the right organizational feature will unlock that novel hidden in their soul. Meanwhile, the paper stays blank, matching the expression on the would-be writer's face.

Truth bomb: The tool you use to write is not going to magically turn you into Mark Twain. You could write in Microsoft Word, Google Docs, Scrivener, Notepad, a typewriter, a slab of stone with a chisel—whatever. It's not about the tool; it's about the time you spend actually putting words down. If you find an app that helps you stay focused and you genuinely use it, great. But don't let the search for that "perfect software solution" become your creative black hole. All you need is something that lets you type and save your work or ink that isn't invisible. Period. The rest is gravy.

3. Notebooks, Pens, and Other Precious Artifacts

If the digital realm is a circus, the analog realm is a boutique shop with overpriced candles. Let's talk about those fancy notebooks that cost more than your monthly phone bill. You know, the ones with the buttery pages that apparently inspire you to "journal your heart out." Or the pens that promise "an unparalleled writing experience," as though they hold the key to a parallel universe where you're a best-selling author and Stephen King is your typist.

Here's the deal: a notebook is just paper. A pen is just ink. If you enjoy writing by hand, by all means, do it. Some folks genuinely connect better with the page that way. I do. I write everything by hand, and I find that there's a certain unfiltered stream-of-consciousness that can come from scribbling. Plus, I can't type for shit. My pens come in a package of 10 and my paper is white and cheap and usually ends up with some sort of stain on it, coffee, diet pop or some food substance. *Please*, let's not pretend the brand or the cost matters. You can outline a masterpiece on the back of a napkin if you really want to. Great ideas aren't snobs. They don't look at your cheap pen and say, "Nope, I only flow when you use the Montblanc."

Beware of turning your stationery into another barrier. "I can't write today because I ran out of my special Japanese calligraphy paper." Oh yeah, people say stuff like that. That's just more creative avoidance. If you're in the mood to write, use the nearest piece of paper. Hell, use a paper towel if you have to. Because if you're waiting on the perfect pen, you're just letting good ideas die in the swirling vortex of your daily inertia.

4. Desk Toys and Distractions

Now, let's turn to the tchotchkes. Hell of a word isn't it. Yes, it's those adorable stress balls, bobbleheads, and shiny ornaments cluttering your workspace. Maybe you've got an "inspirational" plaque that says something trite like, "Shoot for the moon. Even if you miss, you'll land among the stars." Right. Because we live in a galaxy of participation trophies, I guess. Everyone wins. Bullshit.

Desk toys can be fun. They can even be beneficial if they help you fidget and think. But often, they're just one more extension of *stuff*. One more reason to not be writing. Picture this: You've sat down to finally work on Chapter Six, but you notice your lucky troll doll is a bit dusty. Better clean it. And while you're at it, rearrange all your books by color on the shelf behind you. Suddenly, it's 10 p.m., and you've spent the whole evening playing interior decorator to your workspace. Chapter Six is still inside the uncracked shell.

I'm not saying you should work in a sterile, personality-free cell. But if you find yourself rearranging your Funko Pop collection more often than writing, those figurines are a distraction, not a decoration. L.Roy would say something like, "You wanna write? Write. You wanna play with dolls? That's a different hobby." If you prefer the dolls ….well, anyway, moving along.

5. Expensive Writing Retreats (a.k.a. Paid Procrastination)

Have you heard about these "exclusive writing retreats" where you pay a small fortune to stay in a cabin or a castle or on a remote island? The brochure promises uninterrupted creative time, daily yoga, and "transformative group sessions." Apparently, you'll find your muse *and* fix your chakras, all for the low, low price of an Ivy League college tuition. Look, if you can afford it and genuinely enjoy it, knock yourself out. You might even hook up with another frustrated author in the making. It could happen. But don't con yourself into believing that plunking down thousands of dollars is a prerequisite for putting words on paper. I'm telling you, people go for this shit. I've often thought of putting a couple of tents in my backyard and printing brochures that promise aspiring authors a chance to interact with the spirits of Truman Capote, Anne Perry and Harvey Kurtzman from Mad Magazine, who have all reincarnated into two possums and a three-legged squirrel that live in my shed. Hey, don't bet against getting takers.

But you don't need a fancy retreat to write. You need focus. You need to decide that your writing is worth your time, wherever you are. Could a peaceful environment help? Sure, for a while. But if you don't have the discipline to write in your current life, a week at a fancy getaway isn't going to fix that. You'll come back home with a half-finished draft and a completely empty wallet. Then reality will slap you in the face, and you'll realize the same old distractions are still waiting. So before you drop a wad of cash on a mystical writer's haven, consider this: *maybe* you just need to learn how to carve out writing time in the strange life you already have.

6. Library vs. Coffee Shop vs. Your Living Room

Now, if you must search for an alternate space to write, keep it simple. Libraries and coffee shops can be fantastic if you need a change of scenery or if your home is too damn noisy. They're free (or nearly free if you buy a coffee), they have chairs and tables, and the hum of life around you can be oddly motivating. Some people find the background chatter helpful; others need total silence.

But for the love of all that is unholy, *don't* spend weeks dithering over which coffee shop has the perfect vibe. "I like the cappuccinos at Java Joe's, but the seats at Bean Heaven are more comfortable." If you're investing more time in comparing café amenities than actual writing, you're self-sabotaging. Just pick a spot. Sit. Write. If it sucks, you can move on tomorrow.

The same principle applies to libraries. They're quiet, they have desks, and they're full of books if you need a quick reference. But you don't need to systematically evaluate every branch in your city to find the "ideal" library nook. Again, that's advanced-level procrastination.

7. Writer's Groups and Critique Circles: Use Wisely

We should talk about writer's groups and critique circles. These aren't exactly physical tools, but they can become mental crutches or, worse, creative echo chambers that stifle real progress. Don't get me wrong—support from fellow writers can be wonderful. It's nice to have people who understand the misery of rewriting the same sentence 12 times and banging your head on the desk until knots form in frustration. But sometimes, writer's groups become therapy sessions or endless feedback loops that keep you from actually finishing anything.

You might start craving validation like a kid craves candy. "Oh, I can't move on to Chapter Two until everyone approves of Chapter One, I need to be certain of its flow and momentum." Good god don't start spewing shit like that. You'll spend months rewriting Chapter One based on every little comment from the group, while your momentum grinds to a halt. Then, ironically, you'll blame the group for "slowing you down," even though you were the one who begged for feedback in the first place.

If you do join a writer's group, set boundaries. Use the feedback that resonates, discard the rest, and keep writing forward. Don't let your group become a crutch that prevents you from forging your own path.

8. The Real Requirements: Time, Guts, and an Outlet to Write

So, if most of this chapter is about stuff you *don't* need, let's pinpoint what you *do* need:

1. **Time.** You need to carve out some hours—maybe early in the morning, maybe late at night, maybe during lunch—to actually write.
2. **Guts.** You have to be willing to face the blank page and the possibility that the first draft might read like a teenager's text messages.
3. **An Outlet.** Whether it's a word processor, a pen and paper, or a stone tablet, you just need something that captures your words.

That's pretty much it. Sure, you can optimize these conditions a bit if you like. But don't kid yourself into thinking you need an array of complicated gear to get started. Plenty of great authors wrote masterpieces with pen and paper by candlelight or hammered away at a typewriter with sticky keys. You're living in an era where laptops are portable, your phone can act as a mini-computer, and cloud storage can back up your work automatically. If anything, you've got too many conveniences, so stop with the insecurities, already.

9. Stop Hiding Behind the Tool Hunt

"Tool hunting" is what I call that perpetual cycle of searching for the next big thing that will allegedly make writing easier. But writing isn't meant to be easy. It is not simple. It's frustrating, and occasionally exhilarating. No tool is going to change that fundamental reality.

Let's say you do find a tool that helps you structure your plot or track your daily word count. Great. Use it. But once you've spent a reasonable amount of time learning the basics, *get back to writing.* If you find yourself on YouTube at 2 a.m. watching yet another tutorial on how to color-code your characters' emotional arcs, guess what? That's not writing. That's messing around. You'd be better off writing a crappy paragraph than watching a hundred more tutorials that might shave 0.01% of the hassle off your process.

Deal with the hassle. Deal with the chaos. That's part of the deal. George Carlin didn't become an iconic comedian by perfecting the color-coding of his jokes in a special notebook. He honed his craft by doing it, over and over, in dives and clubs and on television, refining each bit until it sparkled with comedic brilliance. You should do the same with your writing: keep going back to the words, keep tinkering, keep practicing—no matter which tool you're using. Besides, the only tool that counts is the one between your ears.

10. On Perfectionism and FOMO (Fear of Missing Out)

Another reason writers hoard tools is the fear of missing out. You see your buddy on Facebook bragging about how this new note-taking system changed their life, and suddenly you think, "Maybe that's what I'm missing!" But you're not missing anything except the willingness to put your butt in a chair and write.

Perfectionism fuels this fear. You're convinced there's a perfect approach, a perfect tool, a perfect method that will guarantee a perfect book. But perfection is a myth. Even the greatest authors of all time had messy drafts, rough edges, and regrets about certain chapters. The only difference is they actually finished. They didn't wait for the cosmos to align or for Apple to release a new MacBook with the perfect keyboard. They wrote anyway, flaws and all, then revised....and sometimes drank a lot.

Perfectionism is just an elevated form of procrastination. You claim you want the best possible outcome, but secretly you're dodging the reality that writing is a process—one that involves making mistakes, rewriting, and wrestling with your own limitations.

11. Streamline, Simplify, Write

So how do you cut through the clutter? By streamlining and simplifying. Choose a single writing tool—a basic word processor or a notebook—and commit to it for at least a month. Turn off your damn Wi-Fi if you have to. Minimize the number of gadgets and distractions on your desk. Set a timer—maybe 30 minutes to start or even 20—and write without stopping to check every beep from your phone. If your cat jumps on your lap, fine, let it purr away while you keep typing. The point is, you're not giving yourself an easy out.

During this focused writing time, resist the urge to tweak your environment endlessly. Don't say, "I need to rearrange the furniture for better feng shui."

That's code for "I don't want to face this blank page." If you keep the rules simple—one writing tool, one place to sit, one block of uninterrupted time—you eliminate a ton of potential excuses. You might be surprised how fast your word count grows once you stop chasing illusions.

12. But What About Editing and Proofreading Tools?

Yes, at some point, you'll need to clean up your prose. Grammar-checking apps like Grammarly or ProWritingAid can be helpful. Spell-check is practically a necessity unless you're one of those rare beasts who can type 90 words a minute without a single slip-up. But don't you dare let editing become another excuse not to finish the draft. Write the draft *first*. Worry about all the polishing and refining once you've got a complete manuscript. When writing, always edit later, not during.

If you start fiddling with editing tools too early, you'll get sucked into the vortex of perfectionism again. You'll rewrite the same sentences endlessly instead of pushing forward to the next page. Save the big editing sessions for later. For now, get the words out. Even if half of them are spelled incorrectly or read like you're drunk, that's fine. You'll fix it in post, as they say in film.

13. The Real Secret: Discipline Over Devices

In the end, it all boils down to discipline, not devices. George Carlin wrote jokes for decades, and he kept at it whether he felt "inspired" or not. Novelists do the same thing. Some days you'll be in the zone and crank out two thousand words that feel like gold. Other days you'll stare at the screen and wonder if you've lost your mind. Either way, you sit down and do it. That's discipline.

No fancy gadget or perfect app will give you discipline. It comes from within. It's that voice in your head that says, "I promised myself I'd write today, so I'm doing it, even if my pages come out looking like a ransom note." You can't buy that voice, you can't download it, and you certainly can't expect to find it at a writing retreat. You cultivate it by showing up and forging ahead, day after day.

14. Conclusion: Write Now, Buy Crap Later (Or Maybe Never)

If you're still clinging to the hope that there's a magical piece of equipment or software that'll make writing easy, let me burst that bubble once and for all: *there isn't.* Writing is as easy as you make it and as hard as you make it, but it always requires effort. You're converting thoughts into words, and that's a messy business no matter which fancy pen or cutting-edge app you use.

So do yourself a favor: before you run out and spend money on a brand-new laptop or the latest brainstorming software, *just write.* Take the technology you already own, open a blank document, and start typing. Use the free note app on your phone if an idea strikes while you're in the waiting room at the dentist. Scrape together the simplest setup possible and focus on the content rather than the container.

Only after you've built a real writing habit—where you're regularly putting words on paper or screen—should you consider upgrading your gear. And even then, do it because you've identified a genuine need, not because you've been duped into thinking a new gadget will unlock your creativity. Spoiler alert: it won't.

Look, the world is full of stuff, and new stuff comes out every week. If you want to be a consumer of stuff, that's your call. You're gonna end up with a lot of shit. But if you want to be a writer, you've got to realize that writing doesn't come from the outside in. It comes from the inside out. The tools are secondary. Sure, they can make the journey smoother, but they can't walk the path for you. You still have to pick up your feet and move forward, one step at a time, word after word.

Take it from a curmudgeonly voice channeling through your head: *Stop drooling over the shiny objects.* Stop waiting for perfect conditions. Stop telling yourself the myth that you need more crap. What you really need is a commitment to confront that blank page, day in and day out, until the damn book is written. That's the only "write stuff" that matters.

So, here we are at the end of Chapter Three, and hopefully, you're a little wiser about the con game of writing tools. It's time to close this book—temporarily, mind you—and open a new document or grab a piece of paper. Write something—anything—today. Even if it's only a paragraph. Maybe a note to a friend. That act, however small, is worth more than all the fancy pens, curated desk ornaments, and overpriced apps in the world.

Welcome to the real "Write Stuff." It's not for sale at any store, because it's already in you—somewhere beneath all the noise, the excuses, and the marketing hype. Use it. Now,

4

"Procrastination: The Fine Art of Doing Nothing Productively"

Let's start with a confession: If you're reading this chapter instead of actually writing your book, congratulations—you're already a master of procrastination. Don't worry, I'm not here to shame you. Hell, I'm the last person who's gonna tell you to "just do it" because I've spent years avoiding tasks like they were rabid raccoons. That's the beauty of procrastination: it's universal, it's creative, and it's a masterclass in self-deception. And if you think we have dealt with procrastination, you're wrong. Distractions and perfectionism are different. Procrastination is in its own league.

You might even say procrastination is an art form—a fine blend of denial, distraction, and a pinch of fear. We dress it up with noble-sounding excuses, or we bury it under the endless tasks that feel *urgent* but really aren't. How many times have you told yourself, "I can't write right now—I need to blow the leaves of the driveway first"? Because that's obviously more important than fulfilling your decades-long dream of becoming a published author. You see how ridiculous this is? But we do it anyway.

In this chapter, we're going to dissect procrastination like a frog in biology class, guts and all. We'll examine why it happens, how it disguises itself as "productive time," and how you can (maybe) harness it, or at least manage it, without letting it sabotage your entire writing project. L.Roy once said, "If nobody saw it, I didn't do it." Well, with procrastination, our motto is more like, "If I'm too busy doing nothing, I can't possibly write." It's time we crack open that lie and see what's really inside.

1. The Root of Procrastination: Fear Dressed in Pajamas

Let's kick things off by addressing the twelve-foot koala in the room: *fear*. That's right. Procrastination is often just good old-fashioned fear sitting in your recliner. Fear that your writing won't be good enough, fear that you'll fail, fear that you'll succeed and become famous. Okay, maybe not that. But there are lots of things writers fear. It's like a broken record looping in the back of your mind. Maybe you actually do fear being successful and becoming famous. Psychologists and such say that the fear of success is frightening and real. Of course, if it's fear it's frightening, that only makes sense. Real? I've never met someone that said "Well, I finally became successful and now I'm scared to the point I piss myself." Personally, I'd like to get that kind of a scare.

Fear rarely shows up wearing a name tag that says "Hello, my name is FEAR." It's cleverer than that. Fear knows it can't just barge in and say, "You suck, so you might as well not try." Instead, it whispers sweet nothings: "You'd be much more creative after you watch that entire Cajun cooking show on PBS." Or "You're too tired to write effectively right now—better study more online on how to write, or maybe just take a nap, yeah, that's it, a nap."

Before you know it, the day's gone, you've inhaled an entire bag of chips, a tub of cheese dip and your word count is still zero. The funny part? You'll call this a "busy" day. You convinced yourself that *something* needed your attention more than your manuscript. That's procrastination's top trick: it doesn't tell you to do *nothing*; it tells you to do *anything but the one thing* you really need to do. Remember that. Procrastination is the justification of substitution. Substituting the worthless for the worthwhile.

2. The Ingenious Ways We Procrastinate

Let's get honest here. We humans have turned procrastination into a science. If you ever want to see some real creative genius at work, talk to a procrastinator. They can conjure excuses out of thin air, justify them with incredible logic, and even find a way to feel self-righteous about it. Just talk to a government bureaucrat, you'll be in the presence of procrastinating greatness. Let's explore some of procrastination's biggest hits.

2.1 "Let Me Just Do Some Research First"

Ah, yes—research. It sounds so legitimate, doesn't it? "I'm not avoiding writing; I'm just researching my topic thoroughly!" Never mind that your book is about your life experiences, and you've already *lived* them. Or that your story is fiction, and you're spending five hours reading about the migratory patterns of Canadian geese even though your novel is set in a desert. Research can be an endless rabbit hole, easily justifiable and complete bullshit.

2.2 "Household Chores Need Doing—Right Now"

Suddenly, you develop an urgent desire to vacuum your entire house, scrub the oven, rearrange the spices alphabetically, and trim your English Setter's toenails. "I can't write in a messy environment and the dog's feet keep clicking on the floor," you say, as though dust demons are conspiring against your creativity. By the time you've finished making your house spotless, and the pet pedicure is complete, you're too exhausted to write anything. Mission accomplished—procrastination wins again.

2.3 "I Should Learn All About Writing Before I Actually Write"

This one's a doozy. You might say, "I need to read three books on plotting, four on character development, and maybe watch a few dozen lectures on YouTube about the craft." Knowledge is power, sure—but writing is a *doing* activity. Consuming endless tips and tricks without applying them is like buying running shoes for couch setting. Unless you actually run with the damn things, they're just expensive slippers.

2.4 "I'll Be More Inspired Later"

Classic. Procrastination knows no better partner than the idea of "waiting for inspiration." Let's face it, if we only did things when we felt inspired, we'd rarely do anything. Inspiration is like a stray cat: sometimes it shows up, sometimes it doesn't, and it absolutely refuses to come just because you've left out a dish of milk. If writing is important to you, you learn to do it even when you're not "feeling it." Yes, we've already discussed this, but it is the biggest anchor around writers' necks.

3. Productive Procrastination: The Devious Cousin

Then there's "productive procrastination," which is procrastination's slick cousin—the one who always has an elaborate cover story. Instead of vegging out, you fill your day with tasks that look impressive to outsiders. Hell, they might even look impressive to you. You're not binge-watching a cartoon marathon; you're color-coding your calendar! You're not sleeping till noon; you're "recharging your creative energy."

The worst part? You actually feel good about yourself while you're doing it. After all, you're not just lazing around. You're being *productive.* The catch is that you're being productive in everything but the one task that truly matters: writing your book. The net result is the same—no progress on your manuscript. But you're lulled into a false sense of accomplishment.

Productive procrastination is like polishing a sinking ship. It might look shiny, but it's still going down. Hear the gurgling?

4. Why We Love to Procrastinate

Have you ever asked yourself why we cling to procrastination even when we *know* it's screwing us over? Well, there are a couple reasons:

1. **Instant Gratification**: Writing is a slow burn. You don't get immediate feedback or rewards. But social media, TV, or even chores can give you a quicker sense of accomplishment. You do the dishes, and boom—they're done. Words on a page? They need editing, rethinking, more writing. It's never *done* fast enough.
2. **Fear of Failure**: If you don't write, you can't fail. Simple logic, right? It's the same reason some people never ask someone out on a date—they'd rather live with the *possibility* of success than the reality of rejection.
3. **Overwhelm**: Writing a book is a big task. Sometimes it feels like you're climbing Mount Everest in flip-flops. You look up at that towering challenge and think, "Eh, maybe tomorrow."

Understanding these motivations can help you yank procrastination out of the shadows. Because once you see the strings, it's harder to be a puppet.

5. Strategies for Taking the Wind Out of Procrastination's Sails

Now, you didn't think I'd just rant about procrastination without offering a few potential solutions, did you? Don't worry, I'm not here to give you some sugar-coated listicle. But here are a few straightforward tactics you can actually use—provided you stop procrastinating about using them.

5.1 The Pomodoro Technique (a.k.a. "Focus in Small Bites")

If you haven't heard of the Pomodoro Technique, it's simple: you work for 25 minutes, take a short break, then repeat. The idea is to commit to writing for a manageable chunk of time, which feels less overwhelming than staring down a six-hour session. Plus, the ticking clock has a way of forcing your hand: "Hey, I can handle anything for 25 minutes, except listening to my father-in-law sing Aerosmith's greatest hits", you tell yourself. It's like tricking your brain into focusing.

5.2 Break It Down into Micro-Tasks

"Write a book" is massive. "Draft chapter one's opening paragraph" is manageable. When you break your writing project down into small, doable chunks, it feels less like an insurmountable chore. Suddenly, you can see the light at the end of the tunnel—one paragraph, one page, one section at a time.

5.3 Set Real Deadlines (Not the Fuzzy Kind)

Be honest: how many self-imposed deadlines have you set and then blown right through? "I'll finish Chapter Two by Friday," you say on Monday, but Friday comes around and you haven't written a word. The problem is, self-imposed deadlines are easy to ignore unless there's some accountability. You need external pressure—like promising a friend or your writing group you'll email them the chapter by a specific date. Now there's a consequence if you slack off: you'll look like a jerk who can't keep commitments.

5.4 Reward Yourself—but Only After You've Done Something

Instead of rewarding yourself preemptively with "research breaks," how about you actually *earn* that Netflix binge? Write a thousand words, get a reward. Finish a chapter, treat yourself to something you like (maybe a fancy pastry or a new book—just don't spiral into 10 new books that you "have to read before writing"). The reward system works better than we like to admit, even for adults. Just make sure you've truly earned it.

5.5 The "Just 5 Minutes" Trick

Similar to the Pomodoro, but even more minimal. Promise yourself you'll write for *just* five minutes. No matter how lazy, tired, or unmotivated you feel, you can handle five minutes, right? Often, once you start, you'll find you can go for 10, 20, maybe even an hour. But if you still can't stand it after five minutes, at least you tried. This is mental judo against procrastination.

6. Self-Awareness: Shine a Light on Your B.S.

Let's get real life for a second: you gotta call yourself on your own bullshit. Because if you don't, you'll keep falling for the same old tricks. "I'll write after I check my email" is not an excuse; it's a red flag. "I'll write once I feel more inspired" is the siren song of tomorrow's regrets. If you never acknowledge these lies for what they are, you'll never break free.

Let's try this: each time you catch yourself getting derailed, write it down. Literally write the excuse you used to avoid writing. You'll start to see a pattern. Maybe 90% of your excuses revolve around "not feeling in the mood," or maybe they revolve around "chores that suddenly became urgent." Once you see the pattern, you can dismantle it. Besides, you wrote it down. That's writing.... sort of.

The beauty of shining a light on your own nonsense is that it loses its power. Think of it like seeing how a magic trick is done—once you know the secret, it's not as mesmerizing.

7. The Art of Doing Nothing... After You Write

Remember, this chapter is called "The Fine Art of Doing Nothing Productively." I'm not saying you should never rest. Rest is crucial. Doing absolutely nothing can be cathartic—like hitting the mental reset button. But if you indulge in that nothingness before you've done your writing, you're basically paying yourself in advance for work you haven't performed yet.

Flip the script: do your writing first, then enjoy your guilt-free sloth time.

You'll be amazed how much better that TV show tastes or that walk through the neighborhood feels when you know you've actually accomplished something. It turns mindless entertainment into a well-deserved reward rather than a method of self-sabotage.

8. From Procrastinator to Producer: A Mindset Shift

Now, there's a fine line between identifying as a "procrastinator" and identifying as a "producer who sometimes procrastinates." The difference? A producer sees writing as something they *do*, not something they *intend* to do. A procrastinator can talk all day about wanting to write but never truly commits.

So how do you flip that switch? By acting like a producer, even if you feel like a phony. Show up at your desk. Write the words. Stop telling people, "I'm going to write a book," and start telling them, "Can you believe this shit? I'm writing a book!" Be enthusiastic about it, not timid. It's a subtle linguistic difference but a powerful psychological one. If you keep calling yourself a procrastinator, you're giving your brain permission to keep the pattern going. If you start calling yourself a writer—state it out loud—your brain might just start believing it.

9. Embrace the Imperfection

One of the biggest drivers of procrastination is perfectionism—or, more accurately, *fear of imperfection*. We'd rather not write at all than produce something crappy. But guess what? Crappy first drafts are a rite of passage. Every writer you admire has produced reams of trash on the way to something great. The difference is they were willing to write that trash in the first place.

Someone once joked about how people always want everything just so— "we've gotta have it so damned perfect." But life isn't perfect, and neither is your writing, especially in the early stages. Accept that your first draft might stink like post workout armpits in August. That's okay. You can't sculpt a statue without a block of clay, and you can't sculpt your masterpiece without that messy first draft.

Once you drop the pursuit of immediate perfection, you remove one of procrastination's prime excuses. After all, if you're willing to be lousy at first, you have no reason not to start. After all, lousy is easy.

10. The Danger of 'One More Thing'

Let's talk about the "one more thing" trap. It's a cousin of productive procrastination, but worth calling out. You decide you'll start writing in five minutes, but first, "one more thing"—maybe you'll check social media, read the news, or answer that text. One more thing leads to another, and another, and soon you're 45 minutes in the hole, your writing time is shot, and you're beating yourself up.

How do you combat this? Shut down the possibility of "one more thing." Disable notifications, close your email, put the damn phone down or maybe even stash it in another room. If you must check something, schedule it: "After I write for 30 minutes, I'll spend 5 minutes checking messages." This puts you in control of your time instead of letting your digital devices yank you around like a dog on a leash.

11. Accountability: Wrangle a Partner (or Group)

Accountability can be a magic bullet. Nothing quite motivates like the terror of public embarrassment. If you have a friend who also writes—or wants to—form a pact. Share your daily or weekly goals and agree to report back. If you miss a deadline, maybe you owe them dinner or a bottle of wine. If you're feeling extra gutsy, you might post your goals on social media, so everyone you know sees whether you succeed or fail.

The point is to create some real-world stakes. Self-imposed deadlines without accountability are like imaginary fences—easy to step over. But when you know someone's waiting for your chapter, or your progress report, you're more likely to force yourself to show up.

12. Stop Romanticizing the 'Last-Minute Miracle'

We've all done it. We wait until the final hour, then crank out something halfway decent under extreme pressure. That "rush" feels exhilarating—like we're some creative superhero who thrives on adrenaline. But here's the dirty little secret: last-minute miracles are usually just barely good enough, if that. You're often skipping the revision process or ignoring glaring weaknesses. Sure, the adrenaline might give you a spark, but it's no substitute for careful crafting over time.

If you really want your book to shine, don't rely on that "I work best under pressure" nonsense. That's a lazy way of saying, "I only work under threat of immediate consequences." You can be better than that. You can create consistent, disciplined effort over days and weeks, refining your craft instead of hoping for a magical burst of genius in a single all-nighter.

13. The Inevitable Guilt Spiral—and How to Avoid It

Let's not forget the guilt spiral that comes after a day (or week, or month) of heavy procrastination. It's like a hangover. You feel terrible for not writing, which makes you want to avoid it more, which makes you feel worse, and so on. It's like mental quicksand—the more you struggle, the deeper you sink.

The only way out is action, however small. The moment you write even a sentence, you chip away at that guilt. You shift from "I'm avoiding my dream" to "I am taking a step." That can be enough to stop the spiral. But if you keep waiting to feel un-guilty before you write, you'll never write. Action precedes relief, not the other way around.

14. Accepting the Inevitable: You'll Still Procrastinate Sometimes

Here's a final reality check: You're human, so you're going to procrastinate. The idea isn't to become some productivity god who never wastes a second. That's impossible. Even great writers in all their glory take time off to do things that weren't "productive."

The real goal is to catch yourself procrastinating and *choose* whether to continue. If you decide to relax for an hour—fantastic! Enjoy it wholeheartedly. But if you're fooling yourself into thinking mindless Facebook scrolling is "research," call yourself out on that. And then decide: "Do I keep scrolling, or do I close the tab and write?" That decision is the whole game.

15. Conclusion: The Fine Art of Doing Nothing (After You Do Something)

So, yeah—procrastination is an art form, a twisted piece of performance art where you're the performer and the unwitting audience. It's sneaky, it's persistent, and it's had a lifetime to perfect its craft. But if you're serious about writing a book over 50, you've got to learn how to push past it. Not eliminate it entirely—*nobody* does that—but keep it from stalling your progress forever.

Remember the key points:

- **Acknowledge your fear.** It's there, and it's fueling your avoidance.
- **Identify the procrastination patterns.** Which excuses do you use most?
- **Use real tactics.** Pomodoros, micro-tasks, real deadlines, accountability.
- **Accept imperfection.** Your early drafts will smell like day-old fish, and that's okay.
- **Write first, rest later.** Your Netflix queue will still be there when you're done.
- **Stay vigilant.** Procrastination evolves, but so can you.

In the end, procrastination is doing nothing—but making it feel like something. You have to flip that script and actually *do something* (i.e., writing) before you dive into that glorious realm of nothing. Because let me tell you, sitting on the couch doing jack squat is infinitely more satisfying when you've already put words on a page. It becomes a rest, not a retreat. A break, not a bailout.

So, close this book—yes, I said it—and open up your writing document. Hammer out some words. They'll probably be awful at first, but guess what? Awful is better than nonexistent. You can't revise a blank page, but you can revise a crappy one. Give yourself permission to produce something that looks more like a landfill than a manuscript and keep at it until you strike gold. That, my friend, is the real art: turning the fine art of doing nothing into the refined art of doing something. Then, and only then, can you happily laze around in your pajamas guilt-free, wondering why the hell you didn't start sooner.

Because if there's one thing worse than procrastinating now, it's looking back in ten years and realizing you procrastinated your life until the very end. Ouch. Remember, "Today is just yesterday's tomorrow." Don't let tomorrow slip through your fingers again. Write now—later is an expensive luxury you can no longer afford.

5

"Writing While Old: The Pros and the Cons"

So, you've hit that ripe age where you can't pretend you're middle-aged anymore. Maybe you're in your late 50s, 60s, or even 70s. Hell, maybe you're pushing 80. And you've decided—some might say *finally*—to write a book. Good for you! Because let's face it, if you wait much longer, you might be writing it from the afterlife, and the royalties are terrible up there.

But before you dive in with your creaky joints and reading glasses, let's talk about the ups and downs of writing when you've got a few more candles on the birthday cake, a few more wrinkles on the eye corners and a few aches in places you didn't know could even ache. Age is a funny thing: society tells you you're "wiser" and "more seasoned," while your body reminds you that you can't eat spicy food past 6 p.m. without regretting it. Writing while old is no different—it's a sloppy cocktail of experience, cynicism, patience, impatience, aches, pains, and maybe a little unconditional love for your own bullshit.

In this chapter, we'll explore the perks—like actually *knowing* a thing or two about life—and the pitfalls—like forgetting those things two minutes later. So, buckle up, Grandma Moses (or Grandpa Moses), and let's roll this arthritic bus straight into the wonderfully foggy world of writing while old.

1. The "I Don't Give a Damn" Advantage

Let's start on a high note: *you* have the ultimate superpower in writing—*not caring what other people think*. By the time you've reached your golden years, you've probably endured a lifetime of disapproval, unsolicited advice, and the occasional downright insult. If someone didn't like how you lived or what you said, you learned to shrug it off. They have their own shit.... they should worry about that. When you're young you can't follow that advice. When you've reached senior status, it becomes your slogan.

This mindset is *gold* when you're crafting a story or penning your memoir. Younger writers often get crippled by fear: "Will my mom hate me for writing this?" "Will my friends think I'm weird?" "Will society judge me if I put BDSM scenes in my romance novel?" But you? You're too old to care and you might not know BDSM even is. Besides, who the hell cares what people think! If you've spent the last few decades surrounded by loud opinions, you've built up an immunity. And your hearing ain't what it used to be anyway.

There's a special joy in that: a freedom to say whatever the hell you want. Write that scorching political satire or that unapologetic family exposé. You've got less to lose at this point and more to *gain* by being brutally honest. Honesty and irreverence? That's the special sauce of writing that resonates. And guess what? Age grants you a license to be irreverent or completely prickish without apology.

The Caveat: Social Circles May Shrink

Of course, being outspoken might shrink your social circle. Some people don't want to hear the unfiltered truths you've been itching to spill. But hey, that's their problem. One of the perks of aging is that your circle *naturally* gets smaller anyway—people move, retire, or drift away, sometimes they drift permanently. So if your candor costs you a few acquaintances, is it really such a big deal? Probably not. Besides, how many of those prudes and pompous asses did you like, anyway.

2. Life Experience: So Much Material, So Little Time

You've survived heartbreaks, divorces, layoffs, medical dramas, rebellious children, maybe even rebellious grandchildren. You've gone through not one, but multiple economic recessions. You've watched technology skyrocket from vinyl records to 8-tracks, to cassettes, to some shit they call streaming you can get from tiny supercomputers in your pocket. You've seen enough changes in music itself to wonder what the hell happened to the actual melody, not to mention how many so-called superstars can mess up the national anthem during nationally televised football games and still get applause.

In short, you've got *stories*. If your life were a suitcase, it'd be bursting at the seams with comedic anecdotes, tragic tales, random observations, and everything in between. Younger writers often struggle to find something meaningful to say. *You* have more content than you can handle. Way more.

The Downside: Sorting Through the Junk

The challenge? Distilling decades of experiences into something coherent. Your memories might feel like a massive, unorganized attic—lots of dusty boxes, old photographs, maybe a couple of skeletons you forgot you'd stuffed into a trunk. Figuring out which stories are worth telling—and which ones are best left hidden—takes time and a strong editorial hand, and maybe a beer or two.

The solution? Think of yourself as a curator. You're picking the best, weirdest, or most significant "artifacts" of your life to display in your writing. Don't try to *force* everything into one story or novel. That's like cramming all your old furniture into a tiny studio apartment. Just pick what fits the narrative you're telling.

3. The Patience to Write (and Rewrite, and Rewrite Again)

They say patience is a virtue, and guess who has more of it than a jittery 20-year-old? *You do.* You've learned that most good things in life come after consistent effort—raising kids, building a career, or simply maintaining a houseplant without killing it. That same skill helps in writing.

You know that a novel won't be completed in a week (well, not a *good* one), and you're not fooled by quick-fix solutions. You're more likely to accept that rewriting a chapter five times is just part of the process. Younger writers might throw a tantrum or get depressed when a draft doesn't sparkle immediately. You? You shrug and say, "Eh, that's how it goes."

The Con: Physical Energy Ain't What It Used to Be

Of course, patience only goes so far when your body is screaming for a nap. Energy management becomes crucial. You can't necessarily pull all-nighters fueled by energy drinks (unless you want your heart to do a Jose Greco tap dance in your chest). Sometimes, you might want to write for hours, but your neck is stiff, your back aches and your ass just can't sit anymore.

The workaround? *Pace yourself.* Write in shorter bursts. Take breaks to stretch, hydrate, or moan about your creaky bones. Use your patience wisely. Minneapolis wasn't built in a day, and your novel won't be either, but that's okay. You can inch toward the finish line at a pace that respects your well-being.

4. Tech Savviness: The Rocky Relationship

Odds are you didn't grow up with the internet. Hell, you might still harbor a love-hate relationship with it. Or maybe you've met technology with open arms—texting grandkids, Face Timing friends, and streaming TV shows on multiple apps. Whichever camp you're in, technology is a double-edged sword for older writers.

Pro: Access to Endless Resources

Want to look up historical facts, synonyms, or rare medical conditions for your plot? Boom—Google it. Need to self-publish on Amazon? Easy-peasy, once you figure out the platform. The wealth of resources online can be a dream come true for a writer with decades of curiosity stored in their noggin.

Con: Learning Curves, Eye Strain, and Distractions

On the flip side, technology can be a headache. Tabs open everywhere. Ads popping up. Eye strain from hours staring at a screen. And then there's the *distraction* factor: you log on to do research and end up reading about the top 10 ways to keep your skin from turning to sandpaper.

If you're not naturally tech-savvy, you can feel overwhelmed or irritated by the constant changes. "Didn't I just update this software last week? Why is there another update? And what the hell are updates, anyway?" You might recall a simpler time when you just typed on a typewriter and that was that. But alas, typewriters jammed and they didn't know interesting crap like the lifespan of a wombat or the distance from Cairo to Fairbank, Iowa (6,255 miles) so you can't blame it all on modern tech. It is now officially necessary.

Bottom line? Use technology as an ally but set boundaries. Limit your time online or set up your computer so you can't just wander into the digital abyss. Your eyes—and your sanity—will thank you.

5. Emotional Maturity: The Ultimate Editing Filter

One beautiful perk of writing while older? You've likely got a better handle on your emotions. You might still have strong feelings, but you're less likely to fly into a rage or collapse into tears over minor setbacks. That emotional maturity can be a huge advantage when writing scenes that deal with complex themes like loss, love, or regret.

You know that life isn't black and white; it's a carnival of gray areas, hidden agendas, and ambiguous motivations. Young folks might write villains who are pure evil and heroes who are pure good, but you've seen enough to know that real people rarely fit into neat moral boxes. Your characters will ring truer, and your conflicts will feel more authentic when you infuse them with the nuanced perspective you've accumulated.

But Watch Out for Jaded Cynicism

Emotional maturity's dark twin is cynicism. After decades of watching people fail, cheat, or disappoint, you might think *everyone* is unfit to breathe. Don't let that bitterness cloud your entire narrative—unless you're intentionally writing a piece of satire dripping with disdain. A dash of cynicism can be funny and relatable. But a novel or memoir that's nothing but scorn can turn off readers. You can't beat up everyone.

The key is balance. Show the good, the bad, and the ugly. With practice you can develop a knack for mocking humanity's stupidity while still being a people-person at heart. Remember, highlight the absurdities but remember that hope and decency can exist, too—even if they're harder to find.

6. Health Hiccups and Scheduling Woes

Let's not sugarcoat it: as you age, you deal with more health crap. Doctor's appointments, pills, physical therapy, maybe even surgeries, not to mention just general aches and pains from physical exertions like looking for the remote or peeking out the window to see what the hell that weird neighbor is doing. If you've got family obligations (like babysitting grandkids or caring for a spouse), your schedule might be as slap happy as a carnival. Writing can feel like a luxury you can't always afford.

Pro: More Flexible Schedules (Sometimes)

If you're retired, you theoretically have more free time. You're not shackled to a 9-to-5 job or the dreaded daily commute. You can choose to write in the morning, afternoon, or whenever your mind is sharpest, and your body is cooperative. That's a huge plus if you know how to *use* it. If you're not retired, you're screwed. No, no, I'm just joking, lighten up a bit. Scheduling might be tougher, but not impossible.

Con: Real-Life Interruptions

On the other hand, retirement isn't always the glossy vacation brochure experience we dreamt it would be. Those health issues will pop up. Maybe enough to put you on a first-name basis with half the medical staff in your city. Or maybe family members assume, "Grandma's free! Let's have her run errands, pick up kids, and watch the dog!"

You'll need to enforce boundaries. Let people know you're serious about your writing time. "No, I can't drive you to the store at 10 a.m.; that's when I'm working on my novel." They might roll their eyes or accuse you of being selfish, but tough shit. You've earned the right to chase your dream. Besides, if you're bitchy enough about it, no one will bug you anymore. I mean, who the hell wants to hang around an obstinate old coot anyway. But don't worry, they'll get over it by Christmas. Everyone wants presents.

7. Legacy: Writing as a Final Frontier

One significant motivation for writing while old is the desire to *leave something behind.* Maybe you want your grandkids to know your story, or perhaps you aim to pass on some wisdom—or at least some entertaining tall tales. This sense of legacy can be a powerful driving force, giving your writing real emotional weight. Or instead, you can just leave them that old quilt that you were given by your great aunt and your leaf collection from 7th grade science. Great memories, I'm sure.

The Positive: A Deep Sense of Purpose

Remember, you're not just writing for kicks. You're writing to *record* something—your life, your beliefs, your fantasies, your ability to roll a joint with one hand while driving with the other and singing along to "Green River." That clarity of purpose can guide you when the writing gets tough. You're less likely to give up on your project because you're not just doing it for vanity; you're doing it to connect with future generations. Maybe even make them scratch their heads and smile when they realize that grandpa was kind of a hell raiser in the old days.

The Trap: Romanticizing It Too Much

On the other hand, you don't want to get stuck in the trap of turning your book into an endless sermon or a laundry list of achievements. If your writing reads like "Grandad's Greatest Hits," your audience—especially younger readers—might tune out. People want stories with conflict, humility, and raw honesty, not just a pat on your own back.

Think of the best memoirs: they're honest about failures and successes, fears and triumphs. They don't gloss over the messy parts. Write the messy parts. Trust me, they'll make your story memorable.

8. Generational Gaps: What the Hell Are Kids Talking About These Days?

If you're old enough to remember black-and-white TV and telephone party lines, full-service gas stations and women hanging out the family underwear on clotheslines, you might feel disconnected from younger audiences. Slang changes every month, technology is unrecognizable from your youth, and pop culture is.... whatever the hell it is..

Pro: Your Perspective Is Unique

Don't let that gap intimidate you. Lean into it. Younger readers might be fascinated by how different the world was just a few decades ago. You can provide context and highlight how certain universal themes (love, fear, struggle, success) don't change, even if the packaging does. If you think about it, there are only a limited number of events that happen to people and even fewer emotions that come from those events. What makes it all different is the current environment and the people involved. So, as the song says, "Don't Fear the Reaper". He's always around, just now he dresses in Ambercrombie & Fitch instead of Tie-Dyes and jeans.

Con: You Could Alienate Younger Readers

If you rant about "these damn kids" every page, you risk sounding like a crabby old fart. That might be entertaining for a while, but it can also grow stale. A little generational gripe can be funny—but if your entire book is a "back in my day" diatribe, you'll alienate a big chunk of potential readers. No one wants to read a bitching session.

Aim for a tone that's amused and insightful rather than purely dismissive. Show curiosity about the modern world, or at least the willingness to poke fun at both the past *and* the present.

9. The Self-Doubt Boogeyman: "Am I Too Old for This?"

Let's address the big mental obstacle: *doubt.* "Am I too old to start writing?" "What if I die before I finish this damn thing?" These questions can creep in like mice in the attic, nibbling away at your confidence.

Here's the harsh truth: there is no age limit on creativity. If your brain is working well enough to string words together, you can write. Look at the authors who published their first book in their 60s, 70s, or 80s. I'm one of them and guess what? It happens a lot more often than you think. And they often *rock* the literary world precisely because they bring a wealth of life experience to the page.

George Carlin performed stand-up until he was 70, constantly updating his material to reflect the world's absurdities. If he'd asked, "Am I too old for this?" we would have missed out on some of his sharpest commentary. So, don't let the calendar be your creative prison.

Yes, Time Is Finite—So Use It

Sure, you might have fewer years left than a 25-year-old, but that can *motivate* you to work faster or more deliberately. Each day of writing is a step toward leaving your mark. So flip the script: instead of letting mortality spook you into inaction, let it kick your ass into gear.

10. Humor: The Best Tool for the Job

Who says you have to write something serious just because you're older? In fact, if there's one thing we can learn from life, it's that humor keeps you young—at least on the inside. Writing while old can be a comedic goldmine because you've seen enough foolishness in your time to fill entire libraries, and only half of it was your fault.

Pro: You've Earned the Right to Be a Smartass

As an older writer, you can get away with wry observations that younger writers might hesitate to make. You can poke fun at the illusions of youth because *you've been there.* You can roast the illusions of old age, too, because you're living them. That authenticity resonates.

Con: Balancing Humor with Serious Themes

If you're writing about heavy topics—terminal illness, familial estrangement, the meaning of life—humor can feel like you're undercutting the gravity of the subject. But that's the genius of comedic relief: it makes heavy topics more digestible. Just don't overdo it. Insert comedic moments thoughtfully, like spice in a dish. Too much can overpower the flavor and probably give you gas.

11. Practical Tips for Writing While Old (Yes, Actual Tips)

Let's transition all these rants to some practical pointers—briefly, I promise.

1. **Schedule Wisely**

- Mornings might be best if your mind is sharp then. Or maybe you're a night owl. Figure out your prime time and guard it fiercely.

1. **Use Tools That Work for You**

- If fancy writing software confuses you, stick to Word or Google Docs. If you hate screens, write by hand. If your hands ache, try dictation software. Adapt to your body's needs.

1. **Take Breaks**

- You're not 20 anymore, so don't push yourself like you are. Short breaks to stretch, hydrate, or rest your eyes can prevent burnout.

1. **Stay Open to Feedback**

- Let someone read your work, whether it's a friend, family member, or writing group. Don't be the stereotype of the stubborn old codger who refuses to take constructive criticism.

1. **Celebrate Small Wins**

- Finished a chapter? Great. Reward yourself with something you enjoy. Life's too short not to enjoy each milestone.

12. Embracing Your "Oldness" in the Writing

One of the biggest mistakes older writers can make is trying to sound young. Don't do it. If you start peppering your manuscript with modern slang you barely understand, it'll reek of desperation, which is another way of saying it will sound as stupid as hell. Use your own voice, your unique experiences, and your generation's vernacular.

An inspired approach wouldn't be to pretend you're 25. It'd be to stand onstage (or on the page) and say, "Look at all the crap I've seen—and let me tell you about it!" That authenticity is *far* more engaging than a forced attempt to be hip.

Channel Your Inner Curmudgeon—Sparingly

Yes, you can channel that curmudgeonly perspective for comedic effect. People love a well-executed rant. But also mix it up with stories of wonder, nostalgia, or genuine warmth. You want to be hilarious when you complain about life's idiocies, but also add a twinkle of humanity that shows you care about people even as you ridicule them.

13. The Joy of Surprising Yourself

One of the sweetest perks of writing while old is discovering you can still learn, grow, and create something new. Just because you've lived a lot of years doesn't mean you're done evolving. Putting your experiences on paper can lead you to insights you never had before.

You might find yourself laughing at memories that once made you cry. Or finally making peace with an event that haunted you. Writing can be therapeutic, a means of exploring your own life story and maybe even reframing it. And that's a joy you shouldn't deny yourself just because you think you're "too old."

14. Dealing with Naysayers (Including Your Own Inner Critic)

Be prepared for a few killjoys. Maybe your adult children roll their eyes at the idea of you writing a novel. Maybe your friends say, "Why would you do that?" Or maybe you've got an inner critic who insists, "This is a ridiculous waste of time. I could be sitting at a coffee shop with my retired friends bitching about gas prices, not enough rain for the garden and listening to Carl complain about pissing ten times a night because of a swollen prostate." Good times.

If people try to put you down, maybe you should say something unprintable in response to them—but in polite company, you might simply say, "Watch me." Because you don't owe anyone an explanation. If writing brings you satisfaction, do it. If you're worried about being "good enough," remember: the only way to find out is to try. I believe failure to try is simply failure.

A Word on the Inner Critic

You've dealt with that voice for decades. Maybe it told you you couldn't switch careers at 40, or that you couldn't learn a new skill at 50. Each time, you proved it wrong or regretted listening to it. Don't let it sabotage your writing dreams now. The inner critic is just the lazy side of you.

15. Conclusion: Write Old, Die Young (at Heart)

So, what's the final verdict on writing while old? It's a mixed bag of pros and cons—but mostly pros, if you ask me. You've got life experience, emotional depth, the "I don't give a damn" advantage, and a sense of urgency that can fuel your progress. Sure, you've got less physical energy and more health hurdles. You might be baffled by modern tech and occasionally slip into cynicism. But guess what? All of that *adds* character to your writing.

Many people have famously found humor in life's contradictions and injustices, no matter their age. They didn't slow down just because some people said someone in their 70s should retire. They kept producing, evolving, and skewering social norms until the very end. Sure, ultimately even Carlin died, but here we are still talking about his humor, because he stayed at it. That's what writing while old can look like: a relentless, irreverent pursuit of truth, humor, and personal expression—even as the clock ticks. I want to point out that I just made a very profound statement. I wanted to tell you that in case you missed it.

If you're still worried about whether you've missed your chance, let me remind you: some folks pick up painting at 80 and create masterpieces. Others discover a passion for photography in their 70s. There's no reason you can't pen your masterpiece now. Age isn't a disqualifier; it's a qualifier—an entire portfolio of experience that can bring richness to your words.

So, take those aching joints, that reading glasses prescription, that battered heart full of stories, and pour it all onto the page. Whether you're cranking out a novel, a memoir, a collection of essays, or even rants about the modern world—do it with the flair and confidence that only a lifetime of living can provide. That, my dear older writer, is the biggest *proof of them* all.

And if anyone asks, "Aren't you too old for this?" just smile and say, "Not old enough, apparently." Then keep writing. Because there's a whole crowd of readers—young and old—waiting to see what wisdom and wit you've got up your sleeve. And that, my friend, is the real fountain of youth: creating new things as long as you're still breathing.

So go ahead, shuffle to your desk, crack those knuckles, and start typing. You're writing while old, and that's exactly how it should be.

6

"The Chapter Where You Start Panicking"

Ah, panic. We've all been there—that sweaty-palmed, gut-twisting feeling that usually sets in right around the time you realize, *"Holy crap, I'm actually writing a book."* It's the mental equivalent of seeing a flashing red light on your dashboard: you're pretty sure something's about to go catastrophically wrong, but you can't quite figure out what—or how much it's going to cost you. Writing panic is special, though, because no one else can see that big red light except you.

If you're at this chapter, it's likely you've tapped into the existential dread that haunts every writer. "Am I good enough? Do I have any idea what I'm doing? Is anyone going to read this? Do I look like Ernest Hemingway?" Let's face it: you're worried that all those hours spent hunched over your keyboard, ignoring your family, or downing excessive amounts of coffee might end up being for nothing. That fear is natural, it's universal, and guess what? It's also *unhelpful* as hell if you let it paralyze you.

But fear not—well, actually, *do* fear, just a little. Fear can be a nifty motivator if you channel it right. In this chapter, we're going to dig into that panic like a freshly dug outhouse hole. (Apologies if you've never had outdoor plumbing.) Because panic is the mind's way of telling you, "Get off your ass, or we're all going down." Let's figure out how to turn that threat into a battle cry.

1. Recognizing the Early Warning Signs

Panic doesn't always start as a full-blown meltdown with sobbing fits and half-eaten tubs of ice cream or empty shot glasses. Often, it begins quietly, like a small fire in the corner of a room. You notice a flicker, maybe smell a bit of smoke, but you think, *Eh, probably nothing.* Meanwhile, the flames are licking at the wallpaper, ready to engulf your entire mental house.

Here are some classic early warning signs:

1. **Sudden Need to Tidy Everything** You've written three chapters, the momentum is building, and then—*bam!*—you decide your desk absolutely must be cleaned *right now*. You'll find yourself alphabetizing your stack of bills or rearranging the pens in your pen holder by color or size, or a sudden need to clean the parakeet's cage, and you don't even own a parakeet. Anything to avoid that blinking cursor reminding you that your plot is a jumbled mess.
2. **Research Overload** At first, you told yourself you'd do a *little* research to make sure your character's job title is accurate. Three hours later, you're reading about 17th-century pig farming in Eastern Europe. Your actual novel takes place in modern-day Chicago, but hey, you never know when those pig-farming facts might be relevant, right? Right?
3. **Browsing "Writing Tips" Nonstop** You can't write because you're too busy reading about *how* to write. Irony alert: The more "tips" you accumulate, the more paralyzed you become, convinced that you're breaking half the rules you just learned.
4. **Random Full-Body Clenching** Sometimes your panic manifests physically—your shoulders tense, your stomach feels like it's hosting an MMA match, and your jaw is clenched so tight you might crack a molar. This is a sure sign that your brain is screaming, *"Pull up! Pull up! Abort landing!"*

If you've caught yourself in any of these states, congratulations: you're well on your way to a good, old-fashioned writer's panic. The key is to notice these cues before they morph into full-on meltdown mode.

2. Understanding the "Why" Behind the Panic

Now that you've recognized the early warning signs, let's talk about *why* you're panicking. Writers panic for a host of reasons, all of which boil down to a delightful cocktail of fear and self-doubt. Let's highlight a few:

1. **Fear of Failure** I bring this up again because it is the big one. You've poured your time and soul into this project, and the thought of it flopping, or worse—never even being finished—looms over you like a vulture waiting for you to keel over. So, you panic, hoping that if you spin your wheels fast enough, you'll magically outrun the possibility of failure.
2. **Impostor Syndrome** A fancy phrase for feeling like a fraud. You worry that you're not a "real" writer, that everyone who's encouraged you was just being polite, and that you'll be exposed the moment your book sees the light of day.
3. **Comparing Yourself to Others** You read a brilliant paragraph in someone else's novel and think, *"I could never write like that."* Of course, you conveniently ignore all the hours, drafts, and editorial help that other author received. Instead, you just assume they sprang fully formed from the womb with a quill, parchment and Thesaurus in hand, ready to produce literary gold.

Understanding the specific flavor of your panic is crucial because each type of fear has a different antidote. You can't address fear of success the same way you'd handle impostor syndrome. Once you know *why* you're freaking out, you can tailor your approach to calm the storm.

Here's a twist for you: sometimes panic is useful. It's like a smoke alarm going off; it might be annoying as hell, but it's alerting you to a potential problem. The trick is not to *live* in that alarm state. You have to use the panic as a signal that something needs attention—maybe your plot, your research, or your sense of self-worth—but then you dial it back down to a manageable level.

How to Turn Panic into Fuel

1. **Acknowledge the Feeling** Don't pretend it's not there. Give it a nod, a salute, and say, *"Thanks for the warning, brain. Let's see what's up."*
2. **Identify the Root Cause** Use the categories above—failure, success, impostor syndrome, etc.—to label the beast. You can't fight a nameless enemy.
3. **Take a Small, Focused Action** If your panic is telling you that your plot's a mess, spend 15 minutes outlining the next chapter. If it's screaming that you're an impostor, give yourself a pep talk or reach out to a writer friend for reassurance. Do something that directly addresses the *actual* concern, rather than letting the panic roam free.
4. **Set Boundaries** Remember, panic is the passenger, not the driver. It can give you warnings, but it doesn't get to steer. You still decide what actions to take next.

My Uncle L.Roy Crow said, "Panic is good when there's a bull charging at you. Otherwise, it's just a bunch of nonsense that causes your ass to sweat." In other words, panic should be short-lived and purposeful, not a permanent mindset.

4. You Realize You Have *No Plot*—Welcome to the Freak-Out Club

Now let's get specific. One of the most common panic triggers hits when you realize your story has no clear direction. Maybe you started writing with a vague idea—something about a detective who loves crocheting, or a post-apocalyptic romance set on a deserted island. A few chapters in, you're flailing, thinking, *"Where the hell is this going?"*

Symptoms of the No-Plot Panic

- You keep writing scenes but have no idea how they connect.
- You skip from one idea to another like a frog hopping across lily pads.
- You have an entire cast of characters, each with a quirk, but none with a purpose, kind of like a family reunion.
- You spend more time daydreaming about new story ideas than actually working on the old one.

How to Turn This Around

1. **Quick and Dirty Outline** Outline the rest of your story in bullet points—nothing fancy. Just map out a possible path from where you are to where you want to end. It might change, but at least you'll have a roadmap.
2. **Simplify, Simplify, Simplify** Maybe you have too many subplots. Kill some of them (not literally, unless it's that kind of book). Focus on the main characters' goals and obstacles.
3. **Ask "Why?"** For each character action, ask why they're doing it. That question often reveals motives and can help shape a clearer plot. If you can't find a logical reason for something, it might need to go.
4. **Embrace the First Draft Chaos** Remember, your first draft is allowed to be shitty. The plot only has to be *good enough* to keep you writing. You can fix it in the second draft.

5. You Realize You Have *No Time*—Cue the Freak-Out Symphony

Time is a brutal mistress. One day you're young, with endless hours to burn, and the next you're over 50 with a million responsibilities—family, finances, health appointments, social obligations, not to mention the constant desire to just *rest once* in a while. Suddenly, you find yourself panicking because you can't see where the writing fits in.

Why This Panic Stings

It's not just about the book. It's about life. You might be thinking, *"I've waited this long to write, and now it's too late.* "That sense of lost opportunity can be crippling. But maybe, just maybe you can get some of that time back.

Strategies for Reclaiming Time

1. **Micro-Blocks** Write in 15-minute increments. They add up. If you do four 15-minute sessions a day, that's an hour of writing—better than zero. Anything is better than zero when trying to accomplish something.
2. **Schedule or It Won't Happen** Just like doctor appointments, schedule your writing. Put it on the calendar and treat it as non-negotiable. Like

paying your mortgage, or eating, or putting new toilet paper on the holder in the bathroom before you need it. Make your writing a staple of your daily life.
3. **Cut the Fat** Evaluate your daily routines. Are you spending an hour scrolling social media or watching mindless TV? And isn't all TV pretty mindless, Bonanza, Gunsmoke and Perry Mason excluded, of course. But think about it. I mean be really honest with yourself. Couldn't you scale that back and devote that time to writing? Hmm.
4. **Harness Your Inner Rage at Time** Channel the anger you feel about not having enough time into a focused energy that demands you write. Use that anger or frustration to drive yourself through the barriers that the clock puts in front of you. You can use frustration with your schedule as writing fuel. Sounds crazy, because it is. But writing can be crazy. Cool, rewarding and crazy. Sounds repetitive, and it is. But it is all WORTH repeating.

6. "I'm Not Talented Enough" — A Masterclass in Self-Sabotage

Talent? Exactly what the hell is that? I believe talent is just the name we give to the intersection of interest and consistent effort. If you love writing and you're willing to work at it, guess what? You *are* talented or at least have the potential to become so. Yet, that doubt creeps in and can trigger a meltdown. We don't do meltdowns here. Melting cheese in the microwave for a fatty writer's break snack is permitted. Brain baking until you quit is not.

Breaking Down the Talent Myth

1. **You've Read Bad Books, Right?** They got published somehow. That alone should reassure you that the bar isn't impossibly high. In fact, I'm not sure there is a bar.
2. **Talent Grows With Practice** Nobody starts out as a polished writer. Even the greats—Hemingway, Morrison, King, your 7th grade English teacher—refined their craft over years. Well, maybe not the teacher, but she was too damn hot to leave off the list.

3. **Beta Readers and Editors Exist** You're not alone. If your raw manuscript is rough, a good editor can help shape it. Beta readers can give feedback. Talent doesn't have to be a solo endeavor.
4. **Action Beats Overthinking** The best way to kill the "I'm not talented enough" panic is to write more. With each page, you gain experience and skill. You start to see where changes can be made, and tiny little tweaks can change a scene from "ho hum" to "Holy shit!"

Remember, everyone has an opinion. Even those wandering jerks that never accomplish anything and like to make sure everyone around them does the same. The question is: are you going to let that jerk be you? Don't be your own worst critic before you've even finished.

7. "What If My Book Offends Everyone I Know?"

Ah, the anxiety of stepping on toes—especially if you're writing a memoir or anything remotely personal. You're terrified you'll reveal family secrets, offend your third cousin, piss off an ex-boss, let your best friend know that you had a fling with their spouse before any of you were married. Or maybe your fiction draws too heavily on real people. Like the creepy overweight window peeper in your book with only two teeth, no hair and the body odor of week-old roadkill, that reminds you of Uncle Gus.... is Uncle Gus. Don't sweat it. Actually, the fear of offending others can be a bit nerve twitching, just follow your gut. Besides, Gus lives in Dayton and can't read.

Reality Check

- **You Can't Please Everyone.** Even if you wrote the blandest, most inoffensive book ever, some folks would still find a reason to gripe. Screw 'em. The bigger picture is much more important, and you my friend are the bigger picture. Let them write their own stuff.
- **Art Is Risky.** Creative expression often rattles cages. That's part of what makes it powerful. So, Rattle away. Or, as the song says "Shake, Rattle and Roll". That ought to do it.
- **Fictionalize or Modify Details.** If you're truly worried, change enough

identifying traits that nobody can say it's them. If you want a small comfort zone, use this. But, remember, this is your story. Treat it that way.

Handling the Fallout

If someone recognizes themselves and gets angry, you have options:

- **Own It.** "Yes, that was based on you, asshole." Or leave off the asshole if it's your elderly aunt.
- **Deny.** "Any resemblance is purely coincidental." (Might be a lie, but it's a time-honored tradition in literature.)
- **Apologize (If Needed).** If you truly feel remorse, you can talk it out. If not, stand your ground.

George Carlin offended people left and right, but he also made millions laugh. The moral here: you can't break new ground without ruffling some feathers. Accept that writing *might* cost you a few relationships—but if they're that fragile, were they worth preserving?

8. When Panic Turns Into Paralysis: The Danger Zone

There's a difference between a healthy dose of panic that nudges you forward and a full-blown trip to the bank of freakouts and hysteria that will freeze you in your tracks. Paralysis is when you've spent the last week staring at the same sentence, rearranging your desk, or sobbing into your oatmeal. It's when you realize you haven't added a single word to your manuscript in days—or even weeks—because the fear is too great, or you're just completely lost.

Signs You're in Paralysis

- You avoid even *looking* at your manuscript.
- You feel guilt and anxiety just thinking about writing.
- You've considered quitting entirely because it's "too stressful."

How to Break the Spell

1. **Permission to Write Garbage** Allow yourself to write badly. Sometimes the only way out of paralysis is to lower the stakes. You can always revise later.
2. **Buddy Up** Get an accountability partner who checks in daily or weekly. Just knowing someone will ask about your progress can break the freeze.
3. **Change Your Scenery** If your writing space gives you hives, try a coffee shop, library, or even your backyard. A fresh environment can reset your brain. Seriously, this is my favorite tactic and one I have used on a regular basis. Quite often I'll go somewhere that provides new scenery before I get stuck. I wouldn't use bars, strip clubs or nursing homes, unless of course you are in a nursing home.
4. **Seek Professional Help** If your panic is part of a larger anxiety issue, talking to a therapist or counselor can work wonders. Writing doesn't have to be a solo mental battle. Of course, this seems a bit extreme, but I do know a writer, a successful writer, who has done just this.

9. The Mid-Book Crisis: "Maybe I Should Just Start Something New"

Oh, you're about halfway through your draft, and guess what? A shiny new idea emerges, all fresh and exciting. Compared to the tangled mess you're wrestling with; the new idea seems infinitely better. You're ready to ditch your current project and chase the new light in the nighttime sky, right?

Stop. Take a Breath.

This is a classic form of avoidance. A new idea will always seem more appealing because you haven't lived with its flaws yet. Every concept is pristine before you actually try to write it.

How to Resist the Siren Song of the New Idea

1. **Write It Down (Briefly)** Make a note of the new idea, so you won't forget it. Then get back to your main project.
2. **Evaluate Your Actual Goal** Is your goal to *finish* a book, or just to keep starting them? Remind yourself that real progress comes from completion, not endless beginnings.

3. **Reward Yourself Later** Promise you'll revisit the new idea once you've got a draft of your current project done. This is like telling your inner child, "Finish your veggies, then you can have dessert."

10. Preventing Panic Relapses: Long-Term Strategies

Congratulations, you've faced down your writing panic—or at least you know how to handle it now. But guess what? This shit called panic is sneaky; it can creep back in the moment your guard is down. The key is building habits and mindsets that keep panic at a manageable level, day after day.

1. Develop a Consistent Writing Schedule

When writing becomes a habit, panic has less room to fester. Regular, bite-sized writing sessions build confidence and reduce the emotional weight of each session.

2. Celebrate Small Milestones

Finished a chapter? Celebrate. Reached 10,000 words? Celebrate. Every mini victory is a chance to reinforce progress over perfection. That way you can "party with a purpose"—acknowledge the accomplishment, then get back to work.

3. Practice Self-Compassion

When you slip up or go through a rough patch, don't spend a week punishing yourself. Acknowledge it, learn from it, and move on. Beating yourself up is just another form of procrastination in a guilt-ridden disguise.

4. Keep Learning, but in Moderation

It's good to improve your craft, but don't become addicted to writing advice at the expense of actual writing. If you read about a new technique or tip, try implementing it in your current manuscript rather than just stockpiling knowledge. Everyone who writes has his or her own style. It's fine to learn from different styles, but let your own style develop. Don't waste time searching for a style, you really do have one.

5. Maintain a Life Outside Writing

If writing is your entire identity, every setback feels like the end of the world. Have hobbies, relationships, and other interests so that your self-worth doesn't hinge entirely on your book. Maybe fishing, or tennis, or going on long walks with your spouse or your friend with benefits, (probably not at the same time), or just having a cold one on the patio....take breaks.

11. Reality Check

My Uncle L.Roy didn't mince words. He said once, "Life's a series of panic attacks separated by short naps, bad coffee and discovering hair growing from your ears." If that's the case, writing is just an extension of life's absurdities. Yes, you'll panic—maybe multiple times a day. But panic isn't the end of the road unless you let it be.

L.Roy thrives on pointing out the ridiculousness of human behavior. Panicking about writing is a prime example of that ridiculousness: you're freaking out over something you *chose* to do. You're basically punishing yourself for deciding to create something. Hell, you might not have even done it yet. It's like crying over milk that wasn't spilt. Let that sink in.

Now, does that mean you should never panic? No. As we discussed, panic can be a spark. But let it be a spark that lights a fire under your butt, not an inferno that burns your entire manuscript to ashes.

12. Facing the Blank Page Again (and Again)

By now, you've probably learned that panic is cyclical. You get over one hump (plot issues, time constraints, self-doubt), only to find another one lurking around the corner. That's the writing process: a series of challenges, each of which can trigger a mini (or major) panic. L.Roy said he once panicked so bad that he threw open his window and jumped. Fortunately, he lives in a small one-story shack.

Forward, March

The only real way to "win" is to keep moving. Write the next page. The next paragraph. The next sentence. The blank page might taunt you, but every word you type is a small victory. Enough small victories add up to a finished draft.

Imperfection Is Normal

Your first draft might look like a Frankenstein's monster of clunky dialogue, plot holes, and questionable pacing. That's normal. It's not a final product; it's a starting point.

Editing vs. Panic

When you reach the editing phase, guess what? *That's* where a lot of magic happens. You'll improve the structure, refine the prose, and fix those glaring issues that made you break out in hives months ago.

13. Conclusion: Panic Is Part of the Ride—But You're Still in Control

Here we are, near the end of the "panic" chapter. If you've read this far, you're either:

- In the throes of panic, devouring every word in hopes of salvation, or
- Procrastinating by reading about panic instead of writing, or
- Genuinely curious about how to manage this universal writer's affliction.

Whatever the reason, let's sum it up: *Panic is an option, not a sentence.* You choose how deeply you dive into it and how long you stay there. It's a fleeting emotion that can fuel or sabotage you, depending on what you do next.

1. **Acknowledge** you're panicking.
2. **Identify** what's causing it.
3. **Act** in a small, targeted way to address the underlying fear.
4. **Don't Let Panic Drive** your decisions—use it as a backseat driver that warns you, not a lunatic at the wheel, cackling and laughing hideously as he drives you into the river.

The fact that you're panicking or are facing some type of anxiety means you *care.* You care about your book, your story, and your ability to communicate it. That's a good thing. That passion is the same force that'll keep you revising at 3 a.m. or plotting on your lunch break.

So, face the weird paradox of writing: you're going to panic, but you can't let it stop you. You'll feel inadequate, but you'll keep going anyway. You'll worry about offending people, but you'll say what needs to be said. And if you can do all that with a bit of wit and irreverence, you'll come out the other side with a grin on your face—and maybe a damn good book in your hands.

Now close this chapter. Seriously, do it. Enough reading about panic. Go write something—anything. Even if your heart's pounding and your mind's racing. Because the only way to truly conquer the panic is to power through it, one keystroke at a time. Like L.Roy would say: *"Get off your ass already—the world's not gonna wait for you to stop freaking out. Besides, it makes your eyes bulge."*

So, what are you waiting for, get to it.

7

"Self-Editing: Cutting the Crap You Fell in Love With"

So you've reached that dreaded but necessary phase of writing: self-editing. In other words, it's time to put on your steel-toed boots, march into the battlefield of your beloved manuscript, and start clearing away the wreckage. The technical name for this wreckage is *the crap you fell in love with*. Yes, those precious lines, scenes, or entire chapters you swore were literary gold but now realize are clogging your story like a wad of hair in a shower drain.

Most writers approach self-editing like they're performing open-heart surgery on themselves—gingerly, with shaky hands, half-afraid they'll flatline at any moment. If you're over 50, maybe your actual heart has already been through enough. But take heart (pun intended): self-editing isn't a death sentence for your creativity. It's a chance to refine your vision and prove to yourself (and the world) that you can handle the truth about your own words.

So, now we're going to slice through the sentimental nonsense and get straight to what matters: *your readers*. Because let's face it, half the stuff you wrote was for your own ego, therapy, or entertainment. And that's fine—until it slows down your story or confuses the hell out of everyone else and makes your family think it's time for a checkup. Let's learn how to cut that crap, shall we?

1. Why Self-Editing Feels Like Betrayal

Remember when you first wrote that one line—a sizzling piece of dialogue or a masterful metaphor—and you thought, *"Holy shit, I'm a genius."* You typed it out, read it over, probably read it aloud to your dog or spouse. And even though your spouse didn't get it and your dog just walked away, you felt like you'd reached literary nirvana. Now you're looking at that same line and wondering why it reads like an obituary announcement.

The Emotional Investment

You invested time, sweat, maybe tears, into every sentence. Telling yourself now that some of those sentences need to go is like admitting you didn't pick the cutest puppy in the litter. It hurts your pride. But your story's clarity matters more than your ego. *That's the bottom line. Period.*

The Delusion of "But It's So Good!"

Often, you remember how a line *felt* when you wrote it rather than how it reads to a stranger. Your memory is laced with the thrill of creation. But your readers don't have that emotional context. They see only the words on the page. If those words don't serve the story, no amount of sentimental attachment will fix it.

Even the most accomplished authors cut entire bits from their manuscripts if they didn't land well, no matter how much they personally like them. That's the key: If it doesn't serve the show, it's out. Same applies here.

2. The "Kill Your Darlings" Mantra (And Why It's True)

By now, you've probably heard the phrase "kill your darlings." It's the concept that you need to chop out the parts of your writing you love the most—because they're often the pieces that don't actually *belong*. They stand out like peacocks in a flock of pigeons. They call too much attention to themselves, overshadowing what you *should* be focusing on.

What Makes a "Darling"?

- **Overly Flowery Language** You crammed every thesaurus entry into a single sentence to sound "poetic." Except now it reads like a parody of Shakespeare being read by Mr. Rogers.

- **Tangential Anecdotes** You thought it'd be fun to insert that hilarious side story about Aunt Marge's ill-fated casserole, but it derails the plot.
- **Character Quirks with No Payoff** You gave a side character an obsession with collecting bottle caps, but it never affects the story. It's just there, hogging word count.
- **Inside Jokes** You might laugh your butt off at your own inside references, but your reader will be scratching their head, but only until they quit reading.

How to Identify Them

A good test: Ask yourself if the line, scene, or detail advances the plot, reveals character depth, or enriches the theme. If it doesn't do at least one of these, it's probably a darling—one that needs to face the chopping block.

And don't worry. You don't have to delete these darlings forever. That's why we have a magical place called the "cut file" or "outtakes folder," where you can store them for potential use somewhere else—or just visit them fondly when you're feeling nostalgic and need a hug.

3. Approaching Your Manuscript with a Critical Eye

Self-editing demands you shift from being the "proud parent" of your book to being the "tough teacher" who won't let lazy mistakes slide. You have to find a way to read your own words as if they were written by someone else—preferably someone you don't mind criticizing.

Step Away, Then Come Back

If possible, take a short break from your manuscript before you edit—maybe a week or two. Yes, I know you're eager, but a little distance helps you see your work with fresher eyes. It's like stepping back from a painting. Suddenly, you spot the awkward brushstrokes you missed before.

Read It Aloud

Reading your work aloud is a brutal but highly effective method. Clunky sentences will trip up your tongue, and forced dialogue will sound just that.... forced. Your job is to become a master at verbal delivery—know how words flow or get stuck. If you can't read a line without stumbling, that line probably needs reworking.

Consider Hiring an Editor—or a Trusted Beta Reader

Self-editing doesn't mean you have to do it all alone. Sometimes you need an outside perspective to confirm you're not crazy. Just make sure the person you ask has some semblance of taste and isn't afraid to give honest feedback. A "yes-man" or someone who "doesn't want to hurt your feelings" won't help you at this stage. You need a truthful eye poker, here.

4. Avoiding the "Grammar Nazi" Trap

Yes, grammar is important. But some writers get so bogged down in grammar rules that they lose the spark of their writing. If you're writing fiction, for example, sometimes you'll break a rule for style or to reflect a character's voice. That's okay—*as long as it's intentional.*

The Difference Between Errors and Style Choices

- **Errors** are mistakes that distract or confuse the reader: missing punctuation, awkward phrasing, or run-on sentences that make zero sense.
- **Style Choices** are deliberate variations from standard grammar to enhance the narrative. Think of a character who speaks in fragments, or a comedic bit that uses repetition for effect.

Beware the Grammar SWAT Team

If you share your draft with people who treat every violation of standard English as a capital offense, you might end up with a manuscript that's grammatically perfect but has all the life sucked out of it. You must learn to play with language in unexpected ways; no grammar cop will let you get away with half of it if they don't see the comedic or storytelling intent. But they will back off immediately when they realize where you're going. It's your job to show them.

5. Trimming the Fat from Scenes and Chapters

Picture your novel like a steak. You want your readers to savor the meaty goodness, not choke on chewy gristle. A common mistake is letting scenes go on too long or including entire chapters that don't pull their weight.

Questions to Ask for Each Scene

1. **Does it move the plot forward?** If you can remove a scene and the plot remains unchanged, that scene might be expendable. Do not stall the story.
2. **Does it reveal key character traits?** If it's just two characters making small talk about the weather, or one character making coffee or tying his shoes, who cares?
3. **Does it build or release tension?** Scenes should escalate stakes or provide a necessary breather. If they do neither, snip away.

Transitions and Pacing

Sometimes the problem isn't the entire scene but how you transition between scenes. If your pacing drags, look at your transitions—are you overexplaining the time lapse or adding filler? Cut to the chase, literally. Modern readers, especially, are impatient. They want you to keep the story flowing.

6. When Dialogue Becomes a Shitshow

Oh yeah, dialogue. It can either sparkle like fireworks or crash and burn like a flaming dumpster rolling downhill. Self-editing your dialogue is crucial because nothing kills reader engagement faster than stilted, unrealistic conversation.

Common Offenses

- **Info-Dumping in Dialogue** "As you know, Bob, we've been working together for ten years at this accounting firm, and you have three kids..." Stop. Your characters wouldn't spew this stuff at each other; you're force-feeding background to the reader. Find another way. It's important to write like your character would talk.
- **Everyone Sounds the Same** In real life, people have different speech patterns, vocabularies, and rhythms. If all your characters speak like

clones, spice it up.

- **Endless Talking Heads** You have pages of back-and-forth dialogue with no setting or action. The reader feels like they're eavesdropping on disembodied voices. Ground the conversation with some physical or emotional context.

The Cure

- **Read It Aloud** (again, it's a game-changer).
- **Condense** long-winded speeches into crisper exchanges.
- **Use Beats**—small actions or descriptions between dialogue lines to remind the reader who's talking and what's happening around them.

7. Exorcising Purple Prose: When Your Language Gets Too Fancy

"Purple prose" is a term for writing that's so ornate and overblown it becomes laughable or tedious. Think of it as writing on steroids: metaphor stacked on metaphor, adjectives piled like a leaning tower of Pisa, all trying to sound "important."

Recognizing Purple Prose

- You use three adjectives where one would suffice.
- You break out the thesaurus to replace common words with obscure synonyms.
- Reading your own sentence, you get lost and forget the original point.

Why We Fall into This Trap

It often comes from a place of insecurity. We worry we're not "literary" enough. But overcompensating can smother clarity. Real genius is in the ability to slice through pretentious crap with plain language. That's the irony: simpler words often hit harder than polysyllabic monstrosities. Hmm, polysyllabic monstrosities. A bit overdone, but you get the point.

Simple Doesn't Mean Boring

Clarity can be powerful. Each word you choose should earn its place. If an adjective or metaphor doesn't add nuance or evoke a specific emotion, kill it. Let your message breathe.

8. Spotting Repetitive Tics and Lazy Writing

One of the sneakiest problems is *repetition*. Maybe you're fond of a certain phrase or descriptor. Or you keep falling back on the same sentence structure.

Repeating Words

For instance, you might use the word "just" or "actually" every other paragraph without realizing it. A quick find-and-replace in your word processor can highlight just how often you do it. Then you can decide where it's intentional vs. where it's just lazy.

Lazy Fillers

Words like "very," "really," or "totally" rarely add anything. They're filler, making your sentences bloated. Hunt them down and see if you can cut them or replace them with stronger language.

Crutch Phrases

Phrases like "for a moment," "at the end of the day," "couldn't help but," or "it's worth noting." They creep in when we're not paying attention. Once you spot them, you'll see them *everywhere*. Slash them or reduce them to a minimum.

9. The Fine Line Between Revising and Over-Editing

Here's a critical caution: it's easy to fall into the eternal habit of editing. You keep tinkering, polishing, rephrasing—never satisfied. This quest for perfection can lead you to editing away the soul of your work.

When to Stop

- **You're Making Changes But Not Improvements** If you find yourself moving the same words around—back and forth—without a net positive effect, take a break.
- **Your Beta Readers Already Approve** If multiple people have read your manuscript and they say it's good (with few critical notes), maybe trust

them.
- **You're Experiencing Burnout** If the mere sight of your manuscript makes you want to set it on fire, you might be over-editing.

There's no such thing as a "perfect" draft. There's only "done enough." Just understand that sometimes you gotta let the sentence stand, warts and all, rather than over-polish it until it loses its edge.

10. Emotional Pain: Grieving for What You Cut

Let's be real: cutting sections you love feels like a small funeral. You might hesitate, hovering over the delete key as if you're about to murder a family member. It's normal to feel that tug of loss, especially if the cut piece has sentimental value.

Coping Methods

- **Save Them in a "Deleted Scenes" File** Knowing you can revisit those darlins might soften the blow. And who knows? You might repurpose them someday.
- **Remind Yourself of the Greater Good** Every piece of fluff you remove makes your story tighter, clearer, more potent. It's worth the sacrifice.
- **Give Yourself a Reward** If you cut something painfully dear, treat yourself to a small indulgence—your favorite snack, a walk in the park, a big old hunk of beef jerky (my favorite).

A unique approach: maybe channel a bit of dark humor. Imagine your precious lines lined up like condemned criminals, each found guilty of clogging your narrative. It can be oddly liberating to see them marched away.

11. Practical Self-Editing Techniques

Let's get more concrete. Here are some hands-on approaches to keep your editing process efficient and (relatively) painless:

1. **Macro Edit First** Look at the overall structure: chapters, major plot

points, character arcs. Fix the big stuff before obsessing over commas. No point perfecting a sentence that might get cut anyway.
2. **Focus on One Aspect at a Time** Don't try to fix plot holes, grammar, dialogue, and pacing in a single pass. Choose one goal per editing round—plot in the first round, character consistency in the second, then sentence-level issues.
3. **Use Editing Tools (But Don't Over-Rely)** Programs like Grammarly or ProWritingAid can catch grammar slips but remember they can't gauge style or nuance. They're *tools*, not oracles.
4. **Print It Out** Reading on paper can reveal errors you missed on the screen. Yes, it's old-school, but it works. Scribble notes in the margins with a red pen if you're feeling dramatic.
5. **Track Changes** If you're working in a word processor, keep "Track Changes" on so you can see how your document evolves. It's reassuring to know you can revert if you delete something by mistake.

12. Developing a Thicker Skin

Editing your own work is just the first step. Eventually, if you aim to publish, an external editor will come along and offer (or insist on) further cuts. This can be jarring if you've never had to defend or ditch your ideas in front of someone else. Some people get royally pissed during this stage. Not a good idea. Be strong and be open to ideas.

Internal Self-Editing Builds Confidence

The better you get at self-editing, the less it'll sting when a professional editor does it. You'll have already honed your instincts, and you'll be open to changes that genuinely improve the story.

Separate Self-Worth from Your Words

Remember, your writing is a product of your mind at a certain moment in time. It doesn't define your entire being. If something you wrote is flawed, that doesn't mean *you* are flawed as a person. It just means you wrote a bad sentence.

Learn to take critiques on your writing without letting it crush your soul, or get you angry enough to cut down the neighbor's rose bushes. It's necessary for a polished final product.

13. Balancing Honesty and Style

Editing isn't just about cutting. Sometimes it's about *leaning into* a style choice. If you write in a very direct, no-frills manner, then own it. If you prefer lyrical descriptions and it genuinely suits your story, keep it—but keep it focused.

Ask: "Is This True to My Voice?"

Cutting the crap doesn't mean cutting the style that makes you unique. George Carlin's comedic style was often described as "vulgar yet brilliant." He never compromised that style for mainstream acceptance. He refined it, made it sharper, but didn't erase its essence.

Your self-editing goal should be to remove what's *unnecessary*, not what's *uniquely you*. The trick is discerning the difference.

14. Knowing When It's Time to Move On

At some point, you'll have to accept that your manuscript is as good as you can make it right now. Self-editing can become an endless cycle if you let perfectionism take over. The best advice? *Finish the edit, then send it to readers or an editor.* See what happens. You can always revise again based on fresh feedback, but don't linger in isolation forever.

The Danger of Stalling

Self-editing can become your comfort zone, a place where you're "still working on the book" instead of risking rejection by showing it to others. If you sense you're using editing as a shield, call yourself out on it. Time to let the world see your work—scars and all.

15. A Final Word: Welcome the Power of the Red Pen

Chopping down the weeds in your manuscript isn't a funeral; it's a rebirth. Every line you remove makes room for the good stuff to shine. Every scene you tighten adds momentum. Every clunky piece of dialogue you fix brings your characters to life.

"SELF-EDITING: CUTTING THE CRAP YOU FELL IN LOVE WITH"

If your writing process is a chaotic, creative spree—self-editing is the discipline that turns that chaos into something coherent. It's not about punishing yourself or disowning your original passion. It's about respecting your craft and your readers enough to say, *"I'm willing to shape this into the best version it can be."*

Sure, you might occasionally feel like you're slicing off limbs. You shouldn't get attached to every limb anyway—it's just flesh, man. The real heartbeat of your book is in the core ideas, the genuine storytelling moments that truly resonate. Everything else is fancy window dressing you can do without.

So go ahead, sharpen that red pen (or rev up the "delete" key), and start hacking away. Embrace the purge. You'll be lighter, your book will be stronger, and your readers will thank you for not subjecting them to your unedited brain spew. Because let's face it: the only thing worse than wading through your uncut manuscript is never finishing the damn thing in the first place.

Cut boldly, edit fiercely, and take no prisoners—except for those precious gems that truly matter. And if you're smart, you'll find a twisted joy in it. Because once you see how much tighter, funnier, and more potent your writing becomes, you'll realize that self-editing isn't just about removing stuff; it's about unveiling the best of what you have to offer.

Now, off you go. You've got some darlings to murder. And yes, that's as delightfully twisted as it sounds.

8

"Publish or Perish: The Harsh Reality"

So, you've written (or at least *almost* written) your book. You've poured your heart, soul, and possibly your retirement savings into it. Now, you're standing at the threshold of the world of publishing—like a wide-eyed tourist gawking at Times Square, overwhelmed by all the flashing lights and the stench of hot dog carts and waiting to get your pocket picked. Welcome to "Publish or Perish," my friend. It's the stage where many a dreamer realizes that putting words on paper was the *easy* part.

You can have a field day here, sort of, because the publishing industry is a buffet of absurdities. On one side, you have massive corporate publishing houses run by individuals who've probably never heard of you (nor care to), and on the other side, you have the wild, lawless frontier of self-publishing, where literally *anyone* can upload their half-baked memoir about raising gerbils in a flat bottom boat on the Mississippi. And then there's vanity press, that carnival barker who promises to publish your book—if you're willing to pay them more than the cost of your car.

No matter which route you choose, there's an undeniable truth: it's going to be a bumpy ride. You'll face rejection, confusion, financial strain, and possibly an existential crisis or two. And that's before you even get to the part where you try to convince strangers to *buy* the damn thing. So, tighten up the boot straps: this chapter is all about what happens when you decide to share your masterpiece—or whatever—with the world.

"PUBLISH OR PERISH: THE HARSH REALITY"

1. The State of Publishing: A Circus Filled with Clowns

The modern publishing scene is like a three-ring circus, complete with juggling acts, lion tamers, and clowns—lots and *lots* of clowns. Except the animals are your hopes and dreams, and the clowns are the gatekeepers.

Traditional Publishers: Gatekeepers in Tuxedos

These guys wear the fancy suits (metaphorically speaking) and hold the keys to your big-time literary aspirations. They have the marketing budgets, the distribution networks, and the clout to get your book into bookstores—assuming bookstores are still alive by the time you finish reading this. But they also have slush piles that reach the moon. The odds of your query even being *seen* by an actual human might rival your chances of winning a stuffed giraffe at the ring-toss booth. A lifelong goal of many, the giraffe, I mean.

Self-Publishing: The High-Wire Act

Then there's self-publishing—a do-it-yourself approach that's equal parts liberating and terrifying. You control everything—editorial decisions, cover design, marketing—so if you succeed, you keep more of the profits (in theory). If you fail, you've got no one else to blame but the face in your mirror. It's like setting up your own trapeze and hoping you remembered to install a net.

Vanity Press: The Snake Oil Salesman

And let's not forget vanity presses, which some might call "predatory publishers." They promise you the moon, but the catch is that you're paying *them*. "Give us $10,000, and we'll print 500 copies of your book!" Sure, that's exactly what you need: a garage full of unsold copies you'll be handing out to distant relatives, homeless people and Uber drivers until you die.

No matter which path you choose, publishing is an arena where the unprepared get eaten alive. If that sounds pessimistic, well, it's also the truth. L.Roy once said, "It's a big club, and you ain't in it." But that doesn't mean you can't storm the gates.

2. Traditional Publishing: Why the Long Wait?

If you're old-fashioned—or maybe just a masochist—you might try your luck with a traditional publisher. This process typically starts with finding an agent. Why an agent? Because many large publishing houses won't even glance at your manuscript unless some agent vouches for you. It's like needing a backstage pass to get into a rock concert, but the concert people won't let you in, except they smoke enough pot they probably won't notice you walk by. Worked for me at the 1974 Aerosmith concert in Waterloo. It's different with publishers. Publishers won't let you in. Publishers probably don't smoke much pot....but they probably should.

Query Letters and Synopses: Your First Date

You'll write a query letter that's supposed to dazzle an agent in about 200 words or less. Think of it as speed dating with your book pitch. If the agent's eyes glaze over, you're dead in the water. If they're intrigued, they *might* request a partial or full manuscript. That's the good news. The bad news? They'll take three months to reply—if they reply at all. They would make shitty penpals.

The Land of Rejection

Rejections are the norm. Stephen King famously pinned his rejection slips to the wall. If you're sensitive, keep the liquor cabinet stocked because each "thanks but no thanks" stings like a paper cut laced with lemon juice. If you do snag an agent, they'll send your work to publishers, who might also take forever to respond. And if they offer you a contract, expect more months of negotiations and editorial feedback. Then, after all that, you might wait a year or more before your book is actually published. If you're over 50, you might be thinking, *"I could be dead by then, or at least to a point I won't even remember writing a book."* Exactly.

Why Do It, Then?

The lure of traditional publishing is still strong. There's prestige, the chance for bookstore placement, possible foreign rights deals, and the dream of maybe seeing your book turned into a Netflix series. Plus, if the publisher invests in you, it might pick up some of the marketing tab. But the frustration and time involved can be a real test of your sanity.

3. Self-Publishing: Everyone's a Star (Or So They Think)

Ever hear someone say, "I can't believe *that* person published a book!"? That's the upside—and the downside—of self-publishing. The barriers to entry are minimal, so if you can format a document and click "upload," you're officially an author. It's like open-mic night at a comedy club; anyone can get on stage, but not everyone should.

Creative Freedom

The biggest perk is total creative control. You pick the cover, you set the price, you decide how to market. No more gatekeepers telling you to cut 20,000 words or change your main character's name to Biff, which is short for.... whatever the hell it's short for. If you want to write a 900-page epic about left-handed badminton playing nudists in Boise, go for it.

You're in Charge of Everything

Freedom is a double-edged sword. You must pay for—or perform—editing, cover design, formatting, marketing, distribution, etc. If you're not a savvy businessperson or you can't afford to hire pros, your book might look like it was cobbled together in a basement. Maybe it was. Readers can smell amateur hour from a mile away, and your masterpiece could vanish in the digital swamp. Hmm, digital swamp.... sounds real weird and just not good.

Success Stories vs. Reality

You've heard of self-published authors who became millionaires. Those stories are like lottery winners; they exist, but they're rare and you'll probably never meet one. Most self-publishers sell a handful of copies—mostly to friends, family, and maybe a few curious strangers. That's not necessarily a failure, though. For some, just holding a printed copy of *their* book is the dream fulfilled. But if you're looking to make real money, prepare for the marketing hustle of your life, if you've ever had a marketing hustle, or a life. Either way, here we go.

4. The Marketing Circus: You're the Ringmaster Now

Regardless of how you publish, there's one universal truth: *you* will be doing a lot of the marketing. Gone are the days when publishers handled promotion while you lounged around in a smoking jacket. Today, even traditionally published authors often have to hustle on social media, schedule signings, and beg for reviews.

Social Media Overload

Facebook, Twitter, Instagram, TikTok, YouTube, Pinterest—pick your poison. Each platform has its own culture, its own content style, and its own brand of trolls waiting to pounce on anything they consider "spammy." Social media will cause you to spend hours crafting posts that say, "Hey, read my book!" in a way that doesn't sound desperate or annoying. Good luck with that. It can and is done, but it is not made for everyone. You need to make yourself one that can-do on at least one platform.

Email Lists and Newsletters

Everyone says you need a "mailing list" because that's the golden goose of marketing. Trying to set one up is easy—just ask people to sign up. Actually getting them to sign up—and stay signed up—is like herding feral hamsters. You'll spend time writing newsletters, delivering freebies, or pleading for loyalty. It's a never-ending cycle of "Look at me!" that can feel downright soul-sucking if you're not into self-promotion. Sounds promising, I'll bet.

In-Person Events

Remember in-person events? Yes, the sweaty handshake, forced smile, "please buy my book" routine. You might do signings at local bookstores, libraries, or conferences. If you're lucky, a handful of people show up who aren't related to you. If you're unlucky, you'll spend an afternoon twiddling your thumbs behind a table while passersby glance at you like you're hawking timeshare packages or used dentures. You could almost compare this to selling Girl Scout cookies door-to-door—except you're not a cute little girl with goodies, you're the middle-aged writer peddling your homemade literary brownies, hoping someone will bite. And sometimes they do—just not as often as you'd like.

5. Reviews and Reactions: The Yippie and the Ouch

It's not enough to just publish; you need reviews. Good ones will help you attract more readers, while bad ones can sting like a thousand angry wasps. And yes, you *will* get bad reviews if enough people read your book. A universal truth: you can't please everyone. It's not possible. The best hope is that the people that don't like your book just ignore it and don't take the time to call you names and make written judgements about your mental capacities and lack of skill. Doesn't mean they're right. Remember assholes abound on earth.

The Five-Star Illusion

Maybe your best friend or your sibling leaves a glowing five-star review. That's nice, but the real challenge is convincing strangers to care. A dozen honest reviews might do more than a hundred forced or purchased ones. Just remember, the more reviews you rack up, the more likely someone will leave a 1-star takedown. Face it, someone always wants to be a jerkwad. I once had such a review of my first book. It was a real jaw kicker that poked my eyes and drove a railroad spike through my little writer's heart. But I noticed that the person didn't seem to know much about my book in his diatribe, so, it became obvious he probably hadn't even read it. He probably hadn't read anything. He just wanted to be a prick, or he just doesn't like me.

Handling Criticism

Reading a scathing review is like being punched in the gut. The temptation is to fire back a snarky reply or to brood for days. Instead, I would advise you to laugh at the absurdity—someone out there spent their time crafting an angry rant about something *you* created. That's kind of a twisted compliment. Let it roll off you. Don't engage in flame wars—nobody wins those. Though I will admit I once critiqued a bad review once because of spelling errors. Yeah, yeah, I know I said ignore that stuff, but there's no absolute rules here.

Embrace the Silence

Some people say that no reviews at all is worse than bad reviews. I think that a tub of B.S. Bad reviews suck. So, you publish your book and *crickets*. That's the harsh reality for many first-time authors: obscurity. Remember, the internet is awash with content. Getting noticed is a Herculean task. But that's your job! Get your ass moving and do it. Just because you can't bank on instant fame, it doesn't mean it can't be reached. No reviews is much easier to challenge than a bunch of bad ones, but both can be beaten.

6. The Financial Reality: Don't Quit Your Day Job (Yet)

Let's talk money. You might have fantasies of quitting your 9-to-5 and living off royalties. Curb that enthusiasm, friend. The average writer makes peanuts—or empty shells. If you want to see real income, you need persistence, multiple books, and a dash of luck. Even then, it might not pay the bills. It absolutely can be done, making money, I mean. First, you need to understand the business of costs and royalties.

Advance vs. Royalties

If you land a traditional deal, you might get an advance—an upfront payment. But unless you're a celeb or a proven bestseller, don't expect enough to buy a summer house. Advances can range from a few hundred bucks to maybe a few grand. Then come royalties, but you only see those after your book "earns out" its advance, which many never do.

Self-Publishing Costs

Self-publishing isn't free if you do it right. You might pay for professional editing, cover design, marketing services, and more. If your book doesn't sell, you could be out a chunk of cash. Are you okay with that? If writing is a hobby, maybe so. If you're banking on a quick ROI, prepare for disappointment. Budgeting your money is just as important as budgeting your time and you need to do both.

Multiple Streams of Income

Many authors supplement with speaking gigs, teaching workshops, or freelance writing. Some build a backlist of five, ten, or twenty books—over time, that can generate a steady drip of royalties. But it's a long game. Quick riches are rare. Keep your day job until you're sure the writing income is enough to cover rent, groceries, and your dog's Milk Bone treats.

7. The Emotional Roller Coaster: Managing Stress, Doubt, and Hope

Publishing can chew you up and spit you out like stale gum. You'll face stress (deadlines, sales figures), doubt ("Am I a hack?"), and fleeting moments of hope when someone says, "Hey, your book changed my life." It's emotional whiplash.

Stress of Promotion

You'll worry about sales rankings, social media algorithms, and whether your Amazon ads are performing. It's like playing a slot machine—feeding it coins and hoping for a jackpot. The stress can be chronic, eating away at your enthusiasm for writing itself.

Dealing with Doubt

After all the rejections, the low sales, or the mediocre reviews, you might wonder if you're cut out for this. L.Roy once said, "Doubt is a sign of intelligence; it means you're paying attention." A little doubt keeps you humble. Just don't let it paralyze you.

Moments of Euphoria

Occasionally, something wonderful happens: a glowing review from a total stranger, an unexpected spike in sales, or an invitation to speak at a local event. These moments are like oxygen. You might think, *Maybe I'm not delusional after all.* Treasure them, because they can fuel you through the dark patches. If you stay on course, you will have these moments if you produce quality and promote properly.

8. The Vanity Press Trap: Paying for Your Own Exploitation

We touched on vanity presses earlier, but let's dig deeper into why they can be such a nightmare. These outfits prey on desperate authors who crave validation. They promise "publishing packages" that include editing, design, marketing—whatever you want—at an inflated price, sometimes an incredibly inflated price. You foot the bill, they do the bare minimum, then vanish once your check clears.

Signs You're Dealing with a Vanity Press

- **Upfront Fees** that are sky-high, with vague explanations of what you get in return.
- **Aggressive Salespeople** who hound you like you're a timeshare lead.
- **No Quality Guarantees**—they'll publish literally anything as long as you pay.

Why Writers Fall for It

The lure of seeing your name on a book cover can be powerful. If you've tried traditional and self-publishing with no success, you might think, *"At least this way, I'm guaranteed a book in print."* But you'll likely end up with an overpriced product that's poorly edited, with a generic cover and zero marketing support.

How to Avoid the Pitfall

A legitimate publisher pays *you*, not the other way around. Self-publishing means you pay for services, but you choose the providers—and you keep control over your work. Vanity presses blur the lines to confuse you. If your gut says something's off, trust your gut. Do your research, read reviews, and don't sign anything in desperation.

9. The E-Book Revolution and Audio Explosion

Okay, let's talk about eBooks and audiobooks—two formats that have shaken up the industry. Like everything else, they offer opportunities and challenges alike. But the opportunities are real, just like the print book.

E-Books: The Land of a Million Titles

Publishing an e-book is relatively easy. Platforms like Kindle Direct Publishing let you upload your file and start selling within days. The problem? You're a tiny fish in an ocean of digital books. You'll need a strategy—pricing, marketing, keywords—to stand out. Being unique is extremely important. You might think being unique is nearly impossible with all the junk floating around, but alas, it is very possible. Very, very possible. Again, it is up to you.

Audiobooks: The Rising Tide

Audiobooks are exploding in popularity, partly because people like to *listen* to stories while commuting or doing mindless tasks. Producing an audiobook can be expensive if you hire a narrator, but it can open a new revenue stream. Or you could narrate it yourself—if you have a voice that doesn't sound like a singing aardvark. Even if you do, it can still work. It's in the delivery. Of course there is always the possibility of stage fright.... wait there is no stage.... but there might be fright. Get over it. It's your stuff, be proud and speak.

The Format Battle

Paperback, hardcover, e-book, audiobook—each demands different production costs and marketing tactics. If you try to do them all at once, you might spread yourself too thin (and too poor). Prioritize. Figure out where your audience is. Finding your audience can be a task in itself. Start with your tastes as far as reading and media. Are you an Instagram person? Facebook? Maybe neither. Thinking of age groups and people with similar interests is a good place to start.

10. So... Why Bother?

By now, you might be asking, *"Why the hell would anyone publish a book?"* That's a fair question. Here's the simple answer: *because you want to.* Maybe you've got a story clawing at your insides, demanding to be let out. Maybe you've got wisdom to share—especially if you're over 50 and have decades of life experience to pour onto the page. Or maybe you just want the satisfaction of finishing something big, even if it only sells a few copies. As you sit right now without a published product, you really do not know how well it can do in the marketplace when it is finished.

The Unexpected Rewards

Publishing can give you a sense of accomplishment, even if the financial return is modest. You might gain a small but loyal audience, meet fascinating people in the literary community, or inspire someone you've never met. You might roll his eyes at the sappiness of that sentiment, but you probably also will admit there's value in connecting with people through words.

It's Not All Doom and Gloom

Sure, the odds are stacked, the competition is fierce, and the outcomes can be brutal. But let's remember that plenty of authors *do* find their niche, build a career, and produce books they're proud of. Even if you don't hit the bestseller list, you might carve out a little corner of the literary world that's yours. And consider this: a lot of the authors that are doing well enough to quit their jobs and maintain or even improve their lifestyles are people you have never heard of. Basic nobodies, except to a group of readers that like their stuff. You won't get 'em all, but you can get some.

11. Strategies for Surviving the "Publish or Perish" Gauntlet

Before we close this chapter, let's talk practical survival strategies:

1. **Set Realistic Goals** Maybe your goal isn't to sell a million copies. It might be to finish the damn book, get decent reviews, or just see it in print. Having a clear, realistic goal can keep you sane when the industry tries

to break you.

2. **Know Your Strengths (And Weaknesses)** If you're a terrible marketer, consider partnering with someone who isn't, or be ready to learn. If you're not tech-savvy, hire someone to format your eBook. Don't try to do *everything* if it compromises quality.
3. **Keep Writing** Don't make the classic mistake of pinning all your hopes on a single book. Write the next one. Each release can bolster the last. Authors who build a catalog often have a better chance of steady sales. Someone likes your new one, they make take a look at your old one.
4. **Build Relationships, Not Just Sales** Network with other authors, join writing groups, attend conferences. You'll learn from those who've walked the path before you, and maybe pick up a few allies along the way.
5. **Pace Yourself** Publishing is a marathon, not a sprint. I truly hate that overused saying, however, it does describe the process. Spamming your social feeds for a month and then giving up won't cut it. You need steady, ongoing efforts—balanced with your actual life—so you don't burn out or burn up.
6. **Laugh at the Absurdity** When you find yourself obsessing over Amazon rankings or weeping at a 1-star review from "BoredReader69," remember this: the world is full of lunacy, and this is just one slice of it. Laughing can be the best therapy.

12. Final Thoughts: Face the Crazy, or Get Out of the Line

"Publish or perish" is a phrase that originated in academia, where professors had to churn out research or risk losing their jobs. In the writing world, it's not that literal—but it can *feel* that way. If you never publish, you might feel like your work "dies." If you do publish, you enter a battlefield where only the determined survive.

So, what's the choice here? Teach yourself to exist with the insanity or walk away. If you truly can't stomach rejection, self-promotion, or the possibility that your mother might be the only person who buys your book—maybe keep your writing as a private hobby. That's okay. There's no law saying every manuscript *must* see the light of day.

But if you're the kind of person who thrives on challenge, who can handle being both the carnival barker and the tightrope walker, then step right up. It's showtime. Sure, you might lose some money, some pride, and a healthy chunk of your remaining hair, but you'll gain stories—stories about the process, about the people you meet, and about yourself.

And if at any point you find yourself gritting your teeth, muttering, "Why the hell am I doing this?"—just remember L.Roy's retort: *"Because this crazy, messed-up world needs more people who give a damn, and that includes you, so quit whining and write the damn book. Or get me a beer and be quiet."*

No guarantees, no safety nets. But, hey, that's showbiz. Now, go forth and publish—or perish, figuratively speaking. Either way, you've got a story to tell, and if you ask me, that's reason enough to give it a shot.

9

"Fame, Fortune, and the Absolute Lack Thereof"

So you've made it this far—congrats. You've battled writer's block, danced with procrastination, murdered your darlings, and maybe even pitched your book to some poor soul who had the misfortune of standing next to you at the checkout line at Walmart. Now, logically, you might be dreaming of the next step: that glorious moment when fame and fortune come barreling into your life like an out-of-control freight train.

Except, well, that train's usually late or more like a rusty old pickup sputtering along a potholed road, stopping to pick up a hitchhiker or two, then meandering off into the uncharted Chicago wilderness without you. Damn hitchhikers.

For every writer who hits the big time—complete with glossy book tours, paparazzi photos, and appearances on talk shows—there are a thousand more who languish in obscurity, selling five copies a month (if they're lucky). But hey, don't despair. If we have taught ourselves anything, it's that life is a cosmic joke, and the punchline often comes when you least expect it. So, open your eyes wide. We're about to dissect the illusions of fame and fortune, the cold-water reality, and the surprising joys that can come even if your big break never does.

"FAME, FORTUNE, AND THE ABSOLUTE LACK THEREOF"

1. The Glittery Mirage of "Making It Big"

Let's start with the dream. You've probably fantasized about it: your book climbing the bestseller lists, your name plastered on billboards, fans begging for your autograph as you casually push a cart through the grocery store. Maybe you've pictured yourself bantering with Jimmy Fallon or Drew Barrymore about the "real meaning" behind your story. Ya know, shit like that.

Why We Fall for the Mirage

It's human nature to crave recognition. We want someone—anyone—to see our work and pronounce it "Brilliant!" or "Groundbreaking!" Writers, perhaps more than most, crave an audience. Otherwise, we'd be journaling in private diaries and burning them in the fireplace. But the difference between wanting an audience and fantasizing about global stardom is, let's be honest, is pretty damn big. Like the Grand Canyon, but not as picturesque.

In the age of social media, we see overnight sensations everywhere. Some random person becomes a TikTok star for dancing in a Walmart aisle, and we think, *"If they can do it, so can I!"* The problem is, for every dancing-in-Walmart success story, there are millions of folks dancing themselves into a sweaty mess with zero viewers. The same principle applies to writing: yes, you *can* get discovered, but the odds often resemble a cosmic lottery.

The Curse of Comparison

To stoke our illusions, we look at the outliers. We read about that self-published author who became a millionaire or the 22-year-old who scored a seven-figure book deal. We ignore the disclaimers: those stories are the exceptions, not the norm. It's like reading about someone who found a winning lottery ticket stuck to their shoe and assuming that should happen to *us*. Hey, it's *possible*, but let's not bet the house on it. But it's always good to check your shoes, just in case.

2. Money, Money, Money: The Myth of the Mansion

What about fortune? Perhaps you've pictured a future where your book is so successful you can buy a mansion, or at least a small condo in the pricey side of town. You think of royalty checks piling up, each one bigger than the last, like an ever-growing stack of pancakes.

Reality Check, Party of One

Like I said earlier, royalties, for most authors, are modest at best. If you publish traditionally and land a small advance—congratulations, you may have enough to finance a modest weekend getaway or put a dent in your credit card debt. If you're self-publishing, you might see monthly royalties that barely cover your Netflix subscription.

Even for authors who get a decent advance, remember that money gets split in many directions. Agents take a cut, taxes swoop in, and you might have to invest some of it back into marketing and promotions if your publisher isn't footing the bill. By the time the dust settles, you're not exactly Scrooge McDuck diving into a vault of gold coins.

But What About That One Author...?

Yes, there are big-name authors who rake in truckloads of cash. Stephen King, J.K. Rowling, James Patterson—the usual suspects. But that's like pointing to Michael Jordan as proof anyone can become an NBA legend. Sure, it *can* happen, but the majority of players never even make it off the bench, or even to the bench.

3. The Harsh, Beautiful Truth: Most Authors Remain Anonymous

Now that we've kicked your illusions down a few notches, let's go deeper. The truth is many authors—arguably the majority—will spend their entire careers without becoming a household name. They'll produce decent books, maybe even great books, but they'll remain in relative obscurity, known only to a small, dedicated group of readers. Hey, hey hey, don't get discouraged on me. Read on.

Why Obscurity Doesn't Suck as Much as You Think

Obscurity comes with freedoms. When you're not famous, you can write what you want without pressure to please a massive audience or outdo your last bestseller. You can explore weird topics, experiment with style, and take creative risks. If it flops, nobody's going to torch you on Twitter for failing to meet unrealistic expectations.

Carlin never backed down from his worldview, even if it meant alienating certain audiences. If you're comfortable not being on every magazine cover, you, too, can say whatever the hell you want in your writing. The advantage of obscurity is that the stakes aren't near as high. You might find that taking those literary chances might be you as yet unpunched ticket to.... who knows.

Setting Realistic Expectations

This is not to say you shouldn't aim high. Pour your heart into your work. Just remember that success doesn't always arrive in the form of a red carpet. Often, it's a quiet satisfaction that you created something worthwhile—something that resonates with *someone*, even if it's just a handful of loyal readers. Loyal readers talk and they brag, and they might bring more readers to the party.

4. Fame's Dirty Little Secret: It Can Be a Nightmare

Let's imagine, for argument's sake, that you *do* become famous. Everyone wants your autograph, your opinions, your presence at events. You can't pop out for a gallon of milk without fans cornering you in the dairy aisle. Sounds glamorous, right? Sure—until it's not.

Privacy? What Privacy?

Fame can be suffocating. That once-cherished anonymity disappears. Suddenly, if you tweet something mildly controversial, an army of trolls is ready to tear you apart. If you set foot in public, people might photograph your every move. Some authors relish the attention, but many find it overwhelming. Some people thrive on the big stage. But they value the ability to retreat, to not be "on" 24/7.

The Endless Pressure to Perform

Once you've hit big success, there's an unspoken assumption that your next project must be *even bigger*. Publishers, agents, and fans start salivating for your next grand slam. That can choke your creativity, turning writing from a passion into a chore. Suddenly, you're beholden to a brand.

Be Careful What You Wish For

I'm not suggesting you sabotage your own success (that would be damn stupid). But if you find yourself thirsting for fame, ask why. If it's just to feed your ego or impress your ex, you might want to reconsider—fame is a hungry beast that devours egos for breakfast. Why am I even talking about fame here? Because it does happen. New stars are popping all the time. I'm just sayin'....

5. Beyond Book Sales: Alternative Measures of "Success"

One of the biggest traps writers fall into is measuring success solely by book sales and public recognition. This mindset can lead to soul-crushing disappointments. Let's broaden the definition, shall we?

Impact on Readers

Maybe your book helps one person through a rough patch. Maybe it sparks someone's imagination or introduces them to a new idea. That's a form of success money can't buy. Just simple written rants, for instance, shape how people view society, make them question norms. You may turn every book into a gold mine, but who knows? You might influence culture.

Personal Growth

Writing a book, good or bad, forces you to wrestle with your own mind. You learn discipline, creativity, and the art of self-expression. Over 50, you might also be connecting the dots of your life experiences, making sense of regrets, joys, and lessons. That's a reward in itself—though not one you can stash in a bank account.

Community and Connections

By writing, you might find a community of fellow authors or passionate readers. The relationships you build can outlast any ephemeral fame. Whether it's a local writers' group or an online forum, forging bonds around shared passions can be deeply gratifying.

6. You're Richer Than You Think (In Non-Monetary Ways)

Let's talk intangible assets. No, they can't pay the mortgage, but they might keep you sane.

1. **Creative Autonomy** – If you're not under contract with a major publisher demanding you churn out a bestseller, you can write on your own terms. That freedom is priceless. Truly priceless. You think it, you write it. That's freedom.

2. **A Lasting Legacy** – Your words will outlive you, floating around in libraries or e-readers for decades. Even if your name isn't on every lip, your work can still find new fans over time.
3. **Fulfillment** – That sense of accomplishment in having created something, anything, from the raw materials of your imagination and life experience.

I think it's important to remember that we're mortal beings who spend a finite amount of time spinning on this planet. The money you earn will fade, the awards might collect dust, but the intangible satisfaction of having *said your piece* is an investment you carry wherever you go—until the cosmic curtain falls.

7. The Cruel Irony of "Making It Big" Posthumously

I just must bring this up. It's like the ultimate shit luck. It's when an artist gets discovered… after they die. Van Gogh sold very few paintings while alive, and now his works are displayed in the world's finest museums. Franz Kafka asked for his unpublished manuscripts to be burned upon his death; instead, they were published, making him an icon.

The Posthumous Boon

It's a bittersweet phenomenon: you don't get to enjoy the recognition, but your art endures. Could this happen with your book? Maybe. But if you're counting on it, that's a grim plan indeed. You won't be around to soak in the accolades. If you believe in the hereafter, you might believe you'll be floating around and able to see all the post life tributes you're receiving. Maybe you'll be a tortured spirit living in some haunted house watching the occupants reading your book and discussing the brilliance of the author while sipping wine and…. who the hell knows.

Live Long Enough to See It

Better to strive for modest recognition *during* your lifetime than pin your hopes on post-death stardom. We're writing *now*, so we can share our ideas while we can still hear people's reactions (good, bad, or indifferent).

8. Coping Strategies for the "Not-Famous-Enough" Blues

So, you launched a book, and it sold... not much. Perhaps your local newspaper gave it a lukewarm review—if they reviewed it at all. Now you're nursing a heartbreak bigger than an ex-lover's betrayal.

Acknowledge the Grief

It's okay to feel let down. You poured yourself into your project, and the world didn't exactly roll out the red carpet. L.Roy would say, "Join the club, it's a big one." Indeed, you're not alone. Writers all over are crocheting self-pity blankets right now.

Refocus on the Craft

Shift your attention from the external validation to the internal process of writing. If you love the *act* of writing, then do it for that reason. Let the marketing and fame anxieties exist but keep them at the periphery.

Plan Your Next Move

Maybe that book didn't explode onto the scene, but you can always write another. Or pivot to a new genre. Or revise and relaunch. The point is, you're not done unless you decide you are. Writing is a journey; sometimes you take a wrong turn, but you can always reroute. Or quit.... quitter. Don't get all up in your feelings, I'm just joking.

Celebrate Small Victories

Did you sell 20 copies? That's 20 people who read your words. That's not nothing. Did one stranger email you saying they loved your book? That might mean more, in the long run, than a thousand sales to faceless customers. Everything is positive in its own way. Did you ever write a report in school you thought was pretty good? Did 20 people read it? Nope. Just one teacher and she probably marked it all with a red pen. Damn red pens.

9. Handling the Unexpected Gift of a Little Spotlight

Now, let's flip the script. Suppose you *do* get a glimmer of fame—perhaps a minor viral social media post, or a mention in a blog with a decent following. Suddenly, you have a surge of interest in your book. You get an email or two from fans. "It's happening!" you think.

Don't Let It Go to Your Head

A small wave of attention doesn't guarantee you'll be sipping champagne with Stephen King. Enjoy the moment but keep working. Hype can fizzle. In a hurry.

Engage, Don't Spam

If new readers pop up, engage with them. Thank them for their support. Start conversations. But don't immediately turn around and spam them with "Buy my sequel!" 24/7. Nurture the connection like a gardener with tender seedlings. If you keep them in your loop, they will be much more likely to read your next book.

Use the Momentum

A spark of attention can be harnessed. Maybe do a promo or a giveaway to capitalize on the interest. Just be mindful that promotional floods can turn off potential fans. It's a delicate dance: letting them know your book exists without suffocating them with sales pitches.

10. The Ultimate L.Roy Perspective: It's All a Cosmic Joke

L.Roy has a knack for cutting through the B.S. and revealing the absurdities of life. If he were to weigh in on the topic of fame and fortune for writers, he'd likely remind us that *none of it matters* in the grand cosmic scale. The universe doesn't care if you sold 50 copies or 5 million. Eventually, our sun will expand, engulf the Earth, and all evidence of your literary achievements will be burned to a crisp.

Comforting, right? Oddly enough, it can be. Knowing that fame is temporary, and fortune is fickle might free you from the paralysis of chasing them. Once you accept the ephemeral nature of it all, you might just relax and focus on doing what you love—writing. So, write quickly before the big bonfire.

Laugh at the Absurdity

Instead of obsessing over why your writing career hasn't soared, laugh at the cosmic joke. You're a tiny speck on a tiny planet in a vast universe, pounding away at a keyboard in hopes some other speck will read your words and be moved. It's both absurd and beautiful.

Find Fulfillment in the Act

If fame and fortune are merely illusions, what's left? The writing itself, the joy of shaping sentences, the exploration of ideas. That's the one thing you can control and savor.

11. Practical Tips for Staying Grounded

1. **Set Balanced Goals** Have a dream (e.g., "I want to be a bestselling author") but temper it with a measurable, achievable goal (e.g., "I want to finish my next book by December").
2. **Detach Ego from Sales** Easier said than done, but try. View each sale or review as feedback, not a personal endorsement of your worth.
3. **Create an Inner Circle** Surround yourself with a few people—friends, family, fellow writers—who keep you grounded. They'll celebrate your wins and commiserate your losses, reminding you you're human, not just a brand.
4. **Diversify Your Fulfillment** Don't rely solely on writing for your sense of purpose. Hobbies, relationships, volunteer work—whatever floats your boat. That way, if your book flops, your entire identity doesn't crumble.
5. **Keep Writing** Always. No matter the sales or reviews. Write because it's part of who you are, not just because you're chasing external rewards.

12. Embracing the "Lack Thereof" Part

We've tackled fame and fortune. Now, let's put the spotlight on the "absolute lack thereof." This phrase might sound depressing, but guess what? It can also be liberating. If you assume you'll never hit it big, you can focus on writing with fewer inhibitions. You can take comedic risks, champion unpopular ideas, or pen an avant-garde piece that defies trends.

You might fail according to conventional standards, but who said those standards are the ultimate judge? Never shy away from provocative ideas because they aren't "mainstream." In the same vein, you can embrace your own weirdness. You can produce something authentic, edgy, or deeply personal—something that might not fly off shelves but truly speaks to the people who *do* read it.

A Strange Type of Freedom

With no illusions of grandeur, you can operate under the radar, do your own thing, and gradually attract readers who genuinely connect with your work. If that leads to moderate recognition, great. If not, you still wrote your truth. That's a win in any cosmic scoreboard that matters.

13. When the Curtain Falls

At the end of the day (or your life, whichever comes first), you'll look back on the time you spent writing. You'll remember the thrill of a breakthrough idea, the frustration of rewriting a chapter 10 times, the sting of rejections, the tiny triumph of selling your first copy to someone who isn't related to you.

Whether you attained a speck of fame, a modest fortune, or absolutely none of the above, the real question is: *Did you enjoy the journey?* If the answer is yes, then you've already won. Most people would likely sneer at the notion of "winning" in a cosmic sense, but you will appreciate that you found satisfaction in a world saturated with nonsense.

The Legacy You Leave

However big or small, your words will outlive you—at least for a while. Maybe your kids or grandkids will find your book decades from now. Maybe someone will stumble upon it in a thrift store and read it, intrigued by the weirdly specific synopsis. That, in its own understated way, is a slice of immortality.

A Final Thought

We live in a universe that's spinning aimlessly, with billions of folks all trying to carve out a little meaning. Writing is your way of shouting into the void, "I'm here, and I have something to say!" or "Check this shit out!" Fame and fortune are just garnishes on the platter. The main course is your voice, your perspective, and the satisfaction of having translated the chaos of your mind into something tangible.

In the grand scheme of things, (another phrase I can't stand, but it fits) cosmic dust we are and cosmic dust we will return to. Whether or not you get famous, whether or not you get rich, is small potatoes next to the simple fact that *you tried*, you created, and you gave something to the world—however few people might read it. If that's not enough for you, well, blame the universe. It never promised a bestseller list.

14. Wrapping It Up

So, here we are at the threshold of reality, staring at a big sign that says, "Fame, Fortune, and the Absolute Lack Thereof." Maybe you'll tiptoe closer to the first two, or maybe you'll firmly land in the third category. That's the gamble.

In the ultimate writer's spirit, the ultimate advice might be: *Don't take it too seriously.* Sure, pour your heart into your writing, but keep a sense of humor about the rest. If you're older than 50, you've seen enough illusions come and go to know that half of the glitz is smoke and mirrors or a little purple haze anyway.

Focus on writing well, improving your craft, reaching *some* readers, and enjoying the ride. If the gods of publishing smile upon you, fantastic. If not, you still did something extraordinary: you made art in a world that often forgets the value of honesty, creativity, and irreverence.

That, my friend, is a kind of success no one can take from you—not even the savage swirl of time. And if, along the way, you happen to strike gold or land an unexpected moment in the spotlight? Treat it like a pleasant surprise, not an entitlement. Then get back to the page, where the real magic happens—famous or not.

After all, in the swirling madness of existence, the real fortune is that you *can* write, that you *want* to write, and that someone, somewhere, might read your words and think, *"Wow, I'm not alone."* That's the kind of wealth that never tarnishes.

So go forth, keep scribbling, keep ranting, keep stringing words together like the borderline lunatic you are. Fame, fortune, or none of the above—your voice matters, if only to prove that in this vast, indifferent universe, at least one speck of dust had something to say.

10

"The Epilogue You'll Skip Anyway"

So here we are at the end of this little literary trip, the final chapter—a place that most readers will just flip past to check if we stuck in some "bonus content." You know who you are: the folks who read the last page first to see which characters die or if the protagonist finally gets laid. If that's you, welcome. You can now pretend you've read the entire book.

But for the rest of you—those brave souls who waded through every chapter about muses, dumpster fires, writing tools, procrastination, publishing illusions, and the sweet promise of zero fame—this is where we wrap it all up in a nice, messy bow. Because, yes, *that's* how we roll around here: we give you a final flourish you probably don't need but might enjoy anyway.

In the spirit of writers past and present, we'll dish out a last helping of brutally honest advice, interspersed with heartfelt but sarcastic gratitude. Because if you've stuck with this entire fiasco, you deserve at least a handful of zingers and some half-baked encouragement.

1. Why We Even Have an Epilogue

Normally, epilogues appear when an author has to tie up some loose ends or indulge in a final victory lap of self-important rambling. Given that we've spent the last nine chapters meandering through your fear of writing, your fear of not writing, your fear of fame, your fear of not having any fame, and all your other little writerly terrors and ticks, you might think *we* have no loose ends left.

Guess what? We do. Because life is weird, writing is weirder, and no matter how many pages we churn out, there's always something left unsaid. Also, if we ended the book without an epilogue, you'd probably complain, "That's it?" So yes, we're giving you *The Epilogue You'll Skip Anyway*.

But let's say you're *not* skipping it. Let's say you're still reading. Let's say you've got an extra five minutes in your day to absorb more sarcasm and (maybe) glean one or two final tips. In that case, *bless you*. You're the reason authors keep writing epilogues—and jokes, and half-assed disclaimers.

2. One Last Look at the Chapters You Probably Skimmed

Let's do a quick recap of the train wreck you've just witnessed (or skimmed). Because if Carlin taught us anything, it's that repetition is comedic—especially when it highlights absurdity.

1. **"The Muse Is a Liar, and So Are You"**

- We told you that "inspiration" is mostly an excuse for not writing.
- You're waiting for a muse? Good luck. She's probably at the bar sipping gin and giggling at your gullibility.

1. **"Your Life Is a Dumpster Fire of Stories"**

- Embrace the chaos. You've endured heartbreak, taxes, weird family feuds—*that* is prime writing material.
- Don't hide your dumpster fire; wave it around like a flaming flag of authenticity.

1. **"The Write Stuff: Tools and Other Shit You Don't Need"**

- We mocked your obsession with fancy notebooks and writing software that's basically a shiny distraction.
- You can write on a napkin if you have to—just *write*.

"THE EPILOGUE YOU'LL SKIP ANYWAY"

1. **"Procrastination: The Fine Art of Doing Nothing Productively"**

- We admitted everyone procrastinates. Stop pretending you don't.
- Also, start writing the damn book—today, tomorrow, or next year. Just eventually *do* it.

1. **"Writing While Old: The Pros and the Cons"**

- You're older, wiser, and you don't have time for anyone's nonsense. That's a huge advantage.
- Also, your back might hurt, and you might forget half your brilliant ideas—so write them down *quickly*.

1. **"The Chapter Where You Start Panicking"**

- Panic is natural, but let it be your alarm clock, not your prison warden.
- Turn your freak-outs into forward motion—channel that anxiety onto the page.

1. **"Self-Editing: Cutting the Crap You Fell in Love With"**

- Yes, you must murder those "perfect" sentences that don't serve your story.
- A "deleted scenes" folder can be your emotional support.

1. **"Publish or Perish: The Harsh Reality"**

- The publishing world is a circus. You're either the jaded clown or the clueless lion tamer.
- Traditional publishing, self-publishing, vanity press—pick your poison, but know the pitfalls.

1. **"Fame, Fortune, and the Absolute Lack Thereof"**

- Most writers won't become millionaires or household names.
- Focus on the satisfaction of actually writing—fame is a fickle mistress, anyway.

And that brings us right here, to the final stretch, where we tie it all in a knife knot in your shoelaces. Or, maybe, just toss one last sarcastic quip your way and blow raspberries at the notion of closure.

3. Final Tips You Probably Don't Need (But We'll Give You Anyway)

Yes, we *are* going to repeat ourselves—because sometimes you need to hear it a second, third, or fourth time before it sinks in. Or maybe we just like the sound of our own voice. Either way, here are some bullet-point takeaways you'll likely ignore, but hey, we tried.

1. **Write Like No One's Watching**

- Seriously, stop picturing an audience or an editor or your judgmental cousin. Just let the words flow.
- George Carlin never toned down his humor for sensitive ears, and your writing shouldn't pander either—unless you *like* pandering, in which case, do it with gusto. Sissy.

1. **Embrace the Suck**

- Your first draft will probably be terrible. That's okay. Revision is where good writing emerges.
- If you're old enough to remember your first disastrous attempt at a new skill—say, riding a bike, parallel parking, or making out—then you know practice eventually leads to competency. Maybe. Hopefully.

1. **Respect the Process**

- The big secret to writing? There is no secret. It's just sitting down, day

after day, banging out words until they form something coherent.
- If you can handle that, you're already ahead of 95% of the population who just *talk* about writing a book.

1. **Know Why You're Doing This**

- Are you writing for money, fame, therapy, revenge, or all of the above? Knowing your motives can guide your choices.
- "I just like telling stories." That's a valid reason.

1. **Don't Let Validation Be Your Only Goal**

- Sure, we all love a pat on the back, but external praise is fleeting. One day, you're a genius; the next, you're a hack.
- If you don't validate yourself for merely getting words on the page, you'll be in for a world of hurt.

1. **Finish Something**

- Even if it's a short story, an article, or 10 pages of drivel—finishing is a discipline.
- Over time, those small finishes might turn into bigger ones (like an entire novel, imagine that).

1. **Stay Curious**

- Read widely, watch documentaries, talk to strangers (safely and don't accept candy), keep your mind open.
- Curiosity fuels writing. Without it, you're just repeating clichés. Carlin built entire routines on curiosity about human stupidity.

1. **Laugh at Yourself**

- Writing can be pretentious. Don't become one of those authors who thinks every word they scribble is anointed by the literary gods.
- Humor keeps you humble. Trust me, you'll need it—especially when your beta reader tells you your main character is dull as an old dishrag.

4. The Heartfelt (But Sarcastic) Thank You

Now, let's do the dance of gratitude. Because if you're still here, reading this epilogue that we've already declared you'd skip, then you deserve a medal. Or at least a crisp high-five and a shot of whiskey.

- **Thank you** for trudging through these pages, nodding occasionally, maybe rolling your eyes a few times, but still turning them. We appreciate you because without readers, we're just talking to ourselves—which, let's be honest, we do anyway, but it's nicer when someone else is listening.
- **We're Grateful** for any writer who approaches the blank page with sincerity and a dash of irreverence. The world is full of "serious artists" trying to make you feel inadequate for using adverbs. Screw that noise. Write how you want. Just write.
- **If You Learned Something**, that's a bonus. We aimed to amuse you, provoke you, and occasionally drop a nugget of practical wisdom. Whether we succeeded is up to you (and your sense of humor).
- **If You're Offended**, that's life. Part of the fun is stepping on a few toes to make a larger point. But hopefully, you're still here, so maybe you like having your toes stepped on.
- **If You're Inspired to Write**, fantastic. That's the real reason we compiled this nonsense: to give you a jolt of cynicism-laced encouragement. Because writing, while sometimes excruciating, can also be liberating, cathartic, and downright fun—even if you never see a dime in royalties.
- **Thanks for Spending Your Time Here** instead of doom scrolling social media, folding laundry, or cleaning the gutters. Let's be honest, the gutters are probably still clogged. But hey, priorities, right?

5. A Fittingly Ridiculous Conclusion

So, this is the part where we box up the entire fiasco, that final flourish to remind you—once again—what you've signed up for. We gave you a step-by-step look at writing: from lying muses to dumpster fires, from editing heartbreaks to publishing illusions, from the unattainable dream of fame to the sweet spot of obscurity. We did it in a tone that we hope you might have enjoyed. And if not, then you try to do better. I'm serious.

At the end of the day, that's writing: an ongoing, messy, exhilarating process that'll chew you up and spit you out, leaving you battered, bruised, and bizarrely grateful. Because in a world that often feels scripted by corporate PR, writing is one of the last refuges of genuine, unfiltered expression.

And you, dear reader, are either courageous, insane or maybe just high enough to consider jumping into this wonderful cesspool. Good luck. Sincerely. You'll need it. But you'll also love it if you can learn to laugh at every curveball.

Now close this book—seriously, that's it. We're done. There's no secret bonus chapter after this, no hidden conclusion, no riddle to solve for a free T-shirt, besides all my T-shirts have holes. All that's left is for you to go and do the thing we've been yammering about for ten chapters: **write**.

Whether you're 25 or 75, whether you have an agent or you're uploading your manifesto to Amazon at 3 a.m in the nude, whether you're harboring illusions of grandeur or you're content to share your words with a handful of friends—just write. Because the only thing worse than writing and failing is *not* writing at all.

So, in the immortal, irreverent spirit of Uncle L.Roy Crowe, let's bid you farewell with a final bite of sarcastic sincerity:

Thank you. Now get the hell out of here and start pounding those keys— just don't blame us when your family complains that you spend too much time in that little room in the back of the house.

The End. (Yes, really. Go on. Shoo.)

www.ingramcontent.com/pod-product-compliance
Lightning Source LLC
Chambersburg PA
CBHW021627080526
44585CB00013BA/884